GOLD

preliminary

PRELIMINARY ENGLISH TEST

exam maximiser with key

Sally Burgess

Jacky Newbrook

CONTENTS

Introduction to the Gold Preliminary Exam Maximiser

The **Gold Preliminary Exam Maximiser** is specially designed to maximise your chances of success in the Cambridge English: Preliminary exam, which is at **B1** level on the Common European Framework of Reference.

The **Exam Maximiser** will help you prepare for the Cambridge English: Preliminary exam. It provides:

- **practice and revision** of the important vocabulary, grammar and skills (reading, writing, listening, speaking) in the Gold Preliminary Coursebook.
- more **information about the kinds of questions** you have to answer in the exam.
- help with techniques you need for exam tasks and **exam-style activities** for you to practise these.
- a section on **common language errors at B1 level** and practice activities in these errors.
- a complete **Practice test** to use before you take the Cambridge English: Preliminary exam.

How can I use the Gold Preliminary Exam Maximiser?

The **Exam Maximiser** is very flexible and can be used by students in different situations.

> **1**
>
> You are doing a Cambridge English: Preliminary course with other students. You are all planning to take the exam at the same time.

You use the **Gold Preliminary Coursebook** in class. Sometimes you do related activities from the **Exam Maximiser** in class but your teacher may ask you to do some activities at home. You may use everything in the **Exam Maximiser** or just parts of it, depending on your needs and the time you have.

> **2**
>
> You have already done a Cambridge English: Preliminary course and are now studying intensively for the exam.

As you have already worked though the **Gold Preliminary Coursebook** or other Preliminary coursebook, you use the **Exam Maximiser** in class.

> **3**
>
> You have a very short time in which to take the Cambridge English: Preliminary exam.

Your level of English is already nearing Cambridge English: Preliminary exam level though you have not followed an exam coursebook. You use the **Exam Maximiser** without a coursebook because you need practice in the exam tasks and how to approach them.

> **4**
>
> You are preparing for the exam on your own.

You can use the **Gold Preliminary Maximiser** by yourself to practise exam tasks. The **Gold Preliminary Maximiser** gives clear guidance in exam techniques, and answers and audio scripts at the back of the book.

What is in each unit?

The **Gold Preliminary Exam Maximiser** follows the structure of the **Gold Preliminary Coursebook**. Each unit provides more work on the language, skills and exam techniques you studied in the Coursebook unit.

There are **Vocabulary** sections which practise the words and expressions you studied in the Coursebook and also introduce some new words and expressions. There are activities including exam-style tasks and also crosswords and wordsearch grids for fun.

The **Grammar** sections have activities that practise and revise the grammar points you studied in the Coursebook.

Speaking sections provide activities in language and strategies to help you with the Speaking paper. You listen to or read examples of candidates doing tasks and complete activities to help your own speaking skills.

Every unit has a **Listening** section and a **Reading** section which give you information about the exam and techniques to use. Many sections have activities for you to practise unfamiliar words and phrases.

There are **Writing** sections, which develop skills required to complete the exam tasks, and tasks for you to write your own answers. You can check your written work against sample answers.

At the back of the book, there is a **Vocabulary bank** and examples of **common language errors at B1 level** with short activities to help you avoid them.

After you have worked through all the units, you can try the **Practice test** at the back of the book. If you do this under timed exam conditions it will give you a good idea of what to expect in the exam itself.

About the exam

The Cambridge English: Preliminary exam is made up of three papers, each testing a different area of ability in English. Paper 1: Reading and Writing is worth 50 percent of the total mark. Paper 2: Listening and Paper 3: Speaking are each worth 25 percent of the mark.

Paper 1: Reading and Writing (1 hour and 30 minutes)

Paper 1 has two sections. The Reading section has five parts (35 questions) and is worth 25 percent of the final exam mark. The Writing section has three parts and is also worth 25 percent of the final exam mark. Each part tests different reading and writing skills.

Reading	
Part 1 Three-option multiple choice	Choose the correct answer from three possible options for each of five very short texts (e.g. notices, emails).
Part 2 Matching	Read descriptions of five people, then match each person's requirements to one of eight short texts.
Part 3 True/False	Read a text which provides information (e.g. a brochure or website) and decide whether ten statements are correct or incorrect.
Part 4 Four-option multiple choice	Read one long text and answer five multiple-choice questions about it.
Part 5 Four-option multiple choice cloze	Complete a short text with text gaps by choosing the correct word from four possible answers for each gap.

Writing	
Part 1 Sentence transformations	Read five pairs of sentences and complete the gap in the second sentence so that it means the same as the first.
Part 2 Short communicative message	Write a short message, e.g. an email or postcard, including three things mentioned in the task. You will write between 35 and 45 words.
Part 3 Longer piece of continuous writing	Choose one of two tasks and write around 100 words. You can either reply to a letter from a friend or write a story using the title or the first line you are given.

Paper 2: Listening (approximately 30 minutes)

The Listening Paper has four parts, with a total of 25 questions. It is worth 25 percent of the final mark. You hear each recording twice.

Listening	
Part 1 Multiple choice (discrete)	Listen to seven short recordings and, for each one, choose the correct picture out of three options.
Part 2 Multiple choice	Listen to a talk or interview and choose the correct answer from three possible options.
Part 3 Gap-fill	Listen to someone giving information and complete six gaps in a page of notes.
Part 4 True/False	Listen to a conversation and decide whether six statements are true or false.

Paper 3: Speaking (10–12 minutes)

There are four parts to the Speaking Test. You will take the Speaking Test with another candidate, and there will be two examiners. One examiner asks the questions and the other examiner just listens.

Speaking	
Part 1 Personal questions) (2–3 minutes)	Answer the examiner's questions about your present situation, past experiences and future plans.
Part 2 Simulated situation (2–3 minutes)	Look at a set of pictures and discuss a situation that the examiner gives you.
Part 3 Extended turn (3 minutes)	Talk about a photograph for about one minute and listen to your partner's description of a different photograph. Both photos will be about the same topic.
Part 4 General conversation (3 minutes)	Discuss a question or questions with your partner. The question(s) will be on the same topic as the photographs in Part 3.

Identity

Grammar

question forms ▶ CB page 7

1 Put the words in the correct order to make questions.

1 your / is / name / what / ?
2 like / you / name / do / your / ?
3 get / how / you / name / your / did / ?
4 spell / your / how / name / do / you / ?
5 like / you / different / would / name / a / ?
6 what / your / name / favourite / is / ?

2 Answer the questions in Activity 1.

3 You are going to read an article called *Choosing a name – why does it matter?* What do you think the answer to the question is?

4 Read the article. Was your answer to Activity 3 correct?

CHOOSING A NAME – WHY DOES IT MATTER?

Many parents find it difficult to choose a name for their new baby but their decision can be very important.

Research shows that the name you give a child can have a long-lasting effect on them because their name can influence the way they think about themselves. For example, if parents give their baby an unusual name or one with a difficult spelling, it means the child always has to explain their name to others. It can also change the way other people think about them.

It is said that 20 percent of parents regret the name they chose for their child. Others said that they later discovered names they liked better than the one they'd chosen. Maybe the solution is for us to choose our own names!

5 Complete questions 1–5. Use one word in each gap. Then match the questions with answers A–E.

1 Why is .... important to choose the right name?
2 How .... a name influence a child?
3 .... is the problem for a child who has a name with a difficult spelling?
4 .... many parents wish they had chosen a different name?
5 .... is the answer to the problem of having a name you don't like?

A It can change the way a child thinks about him or herself.
B It can affect a child for a long time.
C We should choose our own names.
D A child has to explain it to other people.
E 20 percent.

6 **Find and correct the mistakes in the conversation. There are six mistakes.**

Steve: Hi, I'm Steve.

Bailey: I'm Bailey. Nice to meet you.

Steve: Sorry, I didn't catch that – what your name?

Bailey: Bailey.

Steve: How are you spell it?

Bailey: B-A-I-L-E-Y. Are you think it's an unusual name?

Steve: Yes! Where it does come from?

Bailey: I think it's popular in Australia.

Steve: Have you been there?

Bailey: No, I haven't – it's a long way away!

Steve: So who did gave you the name?

Bailey: Actually, it was my dad – he just liked it.

Steve: Are you have any problems with the name?

Bailey: I think the biggest problem is that it can be a name for both boys and girls.

Steve: Do people find that confusing?

Bailey: Definitely! Before they meet me, they think I'm a boy!

7 ▶ 02 **Listen and check your answers to Activity 6.**

8 **Complete the second question so that it means the same as the first. Use no more than three words.**

1 Do you know what his name is?
   What .... name?

2 Do you know where she comes from?
   Where .... from?

3 Do you know where John is right now?
   Where .... right now?

4 Do you know why Christine left the party early?
   Why .... the party early?

5 Do you know whether she has got a middle name?
   Has .... a middle name?

Speaking
Personal questions (Part 1)   ▶ CB page 7

About the exam:
In this part of the exam you have to give personal information and spell your surname. The examiner asks you and your partner different questions on topics like your family, your interests and your plans.

Strategy:
• Learn the alphabet and how to spell your name.
• Prepare interesting things to say about yourself.
• Give more than one word answers.

1 **Complete the examiner's questions with the words in brackets in the correct order.**

1 Where ....? (you / do / live)

2 How ....? (there / you / lived / have / long)

3 Do ....? (like / there / you / living)

4 Who ....? (live / you / do / with)

5 Tell us .... (your / about / family)

6 Do ....? (work / you / a / student / or / are / you)

7 How ....? (you / spell / do / surname / your)

8 What ....? (your / is / time / favourite / day / of)

2 **Match answers A–E with questions from Activity 1.**

A My mother, father and two brothers, who are older than me.

B About three years – we moved there when my dad changed his job.

C It's a nice place – there are lots of things to do, like playing tennis.

D The morning when it's sunny and the birds are singing.

3 ▶ 03 **Listen and check your answers to Activities 1 and 2.**

4 **Write your own answers to the other questions in Activity 1. Try to give some interesting details.**

5 ▶ 04 **In Part 1 of the Speaking test you have to spell your surname. Listen and write the words you hear.**

1 .... 2 .... 3 .... 4 .... 5 .... 6 ....

6 **Some words sound almost the same as other words but are spelt differently. Choose the correct alternative in each question.**

1 *Where / Wear* do you come from?

2 Have you lived *there / their* for a long time?

3 Do you know *weather / whether* Steve wants to come to the cinema?

4 Is Susan *hear / here* yet?

Listening

Multiple choice (Part 1) ▶ CB page 8

1 ▶ 05 **Listen to the recording. For each question, choose the correct picture and put a tick (✓) in the box below it.**

1 Which picture shows the girl's brother?

A ☐   B ☐   C ☐

2 How did the man find out about the football result?

A ☐   B ☐   C ☐

3 What will the weather be like at the weekend?

A ☐   B ☐   C ☐

4 Where will the man go first?

A ☐   B ☐   C ☐

5 What did the girl buy for Julia's birthday?

A ☐   B ☐   C ☐

6 Which television programme does the man want to watch?

A ☐   B ☐   C ☐

7 What will the woman wear to the theatre?

A ☐   B ☐   C ☐

Vocabulary

describing people ▶ CB page 9

1 **Do the crossword.**

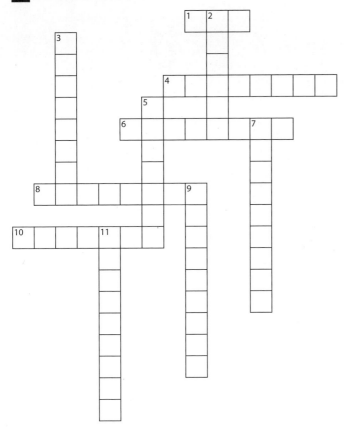

Across

1 I am quite .... when I meet new people – I can never think of anything to say and my face goes red.

4 I'm an extrovert and I'm always very .... and happy.

6 My friend is often late – he's not very .... and never knows what the time is.

8 My sister is very .... and she loves spending her money buying presents for other people.

10 Sam is a very .... person who finds it very difficult to relax, especially before exams.

Down

2 My friend always tells the truth. She's very ....

3 Sue is a very .... person who always does what she says she will do.

5 I'm very interested in finding out about anything new – my mother says I've always been a .... person.

7 I really want to do well in my career – I'm very ....

9 My sister is quite .... Even quite unimportant things can upset her.

11 I make lists of the things I need to do every day. I suppose you could say that I'm quite ....

2 **Write the words in the box in the correct column to complete the table.**

bald   beard   curly   good-looking
handsome   in his twenties   middle-aged
overweight   smartly-dressed   thin   well-built
young

hair/face	age	looks/ appearance	size
....	....	....	....
....	....	....	....
....	....	....	....

3 ▶ 06 **You will hear three people talking about their friends. Listen and match descriptions 1–3 with pictures A–C.**

A ☐   B ☐   C ☐

4 **Complete the descriptions from Activity 3 with words to describe people's appearance. Use one word in each gap.**

1 My friend Janet is .... She's got very pretty .... hair. She's a bit .... so she's always worrying about what she eats.

2 Nick is very .... , in my opinion. He's almost completely .... but that makes him even more handsome. He's quite .... , I suppose, but I find that very attractive too.

3 Tim is quite .... He's probably in his early twenties but he's always very .... Over the last couple of months he's grown a .... I think it really suits him.

5 **Listen again and check your answers to Activity 4.**

Reading

Matching (Part 2) ▶ CB page 10

Matching (Part 2) ▶ CB page 10

About the exam:

In this part of the exam you:
- read eight short texts that describe things like activities, books, films, etc.
- read descriptions of five people (or groups of people).
- match each person to one of the short texts.

Strategy:
- Read about the people first. Underline key information.
- Read through the short texts to find one that matches the first person. Look for key words or information.
- Continue reading the texts and matching the rest of the people.
- Check you have not matched a person more than once.

1 The people below all want to make new friends. There are eight suggestions about how to meet people. Decide which suggestion (A–H) would be the most suitable for each person (1–5).

1 Carla ....
Carla likes working with others to protect the natural environment. She lives in a flat and doesn't like pets.

2 Yuki ....
Yuki studied archaeology but didn't find it very interesting. He works as a journalist and loves reading. He would like to become more confident in speaking.

3 Tara ....
Tara loves travelling but she gets <u>seasick</u>. She enjoys learning about other cultures, especially famous works of art from the past.

4 Daniel ....
Daniel is a big fan of Barcelona Football Club and is quite good at music. When they win, he loves singing the club song with other fans. He isn't interested in his local team.

5 Miriam ....
Miriam is studying psychology. She likes working with children but is also interested in animal psychology and how pets behave. She enjoys doing things outdoors.

WAYS TO MAKE friends

A ▶ Study something.

Why not go 'back to school'? Most universities offer evening or summer courses. You can explore your interests, study for a <u>qualification</u> and get to know the other students.

B ▶ Go to museums.

Many museums have lectures followed by social <u>gatherings</u> where you can meet and talk to people with similar interests. You could also become a volunteer museum guide for overseas visitors – you'll learn a lot!

C ▶ Buy a football season ticket.

If you're a football fan, buy a season ticket for your local stadium. The people who sit near you support your team too but you might have more interests in common.

D ▶ Get a dog.

While out on walks, your dog will 'introduce' you to other dog owners but you could also take him to <u>obedience</u> classes. You'll have a happy pet and some new friends as well.

E ▶ Join a choir.

If you're a frustrated musician, then why not join a choir? Performing will give you a sense of <u>achievement</u> – one you'll share with the other choir members.

F ▶ Volunteer.

Teach teenagers about recycling or help clean up a local beach. You'll feel good about yourself and activities like these are a perfect way of meeting like-minded people.

G ▶ Go on a cruise.

Cruises are a great way of meeting a wide range of people from different countries. There's always a huge programme of activities to do, including art and history, so you really can't help making new friends.

H ▶ Join a book club (or start one!).

Some libraries <u>sponsor</u> book clubs but if yours doesn't, start one yourself. Invite friends and <u>take it in turns</u> to choose a book to discuss – it'll certainly improve your conversation skills!

Vocabulary

deducing words in context ▶ CB page 11

1 **What do you think the underlined words in the texts on page 10 mean? Choose the correct option, A or B.**

1 She gets <u>seasick</u>.
   A ill on boats **B** sad about home

2 You can study for a <u>qualification</u>.
   A good mark **B** certificate

3 Many museums have lectures followed by social <u>gatherings</u>.
   A performances **B** meetings

4 You could also take him to <u>obedience</u> classes.
   A doing what you're told **B** jumping

5 Performing will give you a sense of <u>achievement</u>.
   A belonging **B** having done something well

6 <u>Take it in turns</u> to choose a book to discuss.
   A first one person, then another **B** take responsibility

Grammar

indirect questions ▶ CB page 12

1 **Find and correct the mistakes in the indirect questions. There are mistakes in four of the questions. Tick (✓) the questions that are correct.**

1 Would you mind telling me how many close friends you have?

2 I'd like to know how do you normally meet people.

3 Could you tell me do you use any social networking sites?

4 Can you tell me how do you spell your surname?

5 Do you know how is the name Mercedes pronounced in Spanish?

2 **Here are some questions for the people you read about on page 10. Complete the indirect questions so that they mean the same as the direct questions.**

1 Why can't you get a dog?
   Would you mind telling me .... get a dog?

2 Why don't you find art interesting?
   Can you tell me .... find art interesting?

3 Are you studying journalism?
   I'd like to know .... studying journalism.

4 How do you feel when you travel by boat?
   Could you tell me .... when you travel by boat?

5 Where can you study animal psychology?
   Do you know .... study animal psychology?

Writing

Informal letter (Part 3)
▶ CB page 13

About the exam:

In this part of the exam you are given part of a letter that you have received from an English-speaking friend. In the letter your friend will ask you for some information. You write a reply to your friend, using about 100 words.

Strategy:
- Read the task carefully.
- Plan your letter. Think about what information you should include and what language to use.
- Write your letter. Organise it into paragraphs.
- Check what you have written, especially spelling, punctuation and grammar.

1 **Look at the exam task and the letter a candidate has written. Put the paragraphs in the correct order.**

> This is part of a letter you receive from an English pen friend, Suzie.
>
> *In your next letter, please tell me about your friends. What are they like? What do you like to do together?*
>
> Write a letter to Suzie, answering her questions.

Hi Suzie,

A When you come here next month, I'll arrange for you two to meet. You'll really like each other.

B You said you wanted to know a bit about my friends. I'll tell you about Jo. She's my best friend.

C Jo is a really talented person. She writes really fantastic stories and draws the pictures to go with them. She's a bit of a dreamer, I suppose, but that's because she's so artistic.

D It was great to get your letter. It sounds like you've made lots of friends since you moved to America.

Love,

Candy

2 **Now write your own answer to the exam task in Activity 1.**

The business of food

2

Speaking

Extended turn (Part 3) ▶ CB page 15

About the exam:
In this part of the exam you talk about a photo by yourself for about a minute. Your partner talks about a different photo on the same topic.

Strategy:
- The examiner will tell you the topic of your photo.
- You describe what you can see in the photo. It doesn't matter if you don't know the word for something – you can't ask the examiner but you can describe the object instead.
- You can also say what the people are doing and feeling.

1 Label the pictures with the words in the box.

frying pan	hot dog	kettle	milk shake	oven	saucepan
soft drink	straw				

1 ....
2 ....
5 ....
6 ....

3 ....
4 ....
7 ....
8 ....

2 ▶ 07 You will hear two friends talking about food they like and food they don't like. Listen and match the speakers with the questions. Write *M* (Man), *W* (Woman) or *B* (Both) next to each question.

Who

1 cooks their own food? ....
2 likes healthy food? ....
3 likes eating out? ....
4 likes vegetables? ....

5 enjoys meat and fatty food? ....
6 doesn't like chicken? ....
7 likes fish? ....
8 doesn't like raw fish? ....
9 drinks soft drinks? ....

3 Look at two photos of people eating in different places. Which of the things in the box can you find in these places? Match the words with the photos. Some words can be matched with both photos.

apron	biscuits	bottle of water	bowl
cakes	fork	glass	grass	knife	lake
plate	spoon	table	tablecloth	waiter

4 Read what a candidate said about photo 1 from Activity 3. Find and correct the mistakes.

In the photo I can see a family having a picnic inside. They are sitting around a long table which has a curtain on it. The table is outside near a sea and it is on some grass. The weather is good because everyone is wearing summer clothes. There is a lot of food on the table. There are some breads and a bowl of something – I think it's crisps or breads. There is a big fork in the middle of the table, and plates with food on. On the left there are two little girls who are enjoying the food and they are sitting with their big family. They all look happy.

5 ▶ 08 Listen and check your answers to Activity 4.

General conversation (Part 4) ▶ CB page 15

About the exam:
In this part of the exam you talk with your partner for about three minutes. The examiner asks you to discuss a topic related to your photographs in Part 3.

Strategy:
- Listen carefully to what the examiner asks you to talk about. There are usually two things to discuss (e.g. what you do and what you don't do).
- Listen carefully to what you partner says and respond to their ideas. You should also talk about your own experiences and give your own opinions.
- Don't talk to the examiner. Discuss with your partner.

6 Read the examiner's question. Then match the advantages and disadvantages (1–6) with the places (A–C).

Your photographs showed people eating in different places. I'd like you to talk about places where you like to eat and places where you don't like to eat.

	advantage	disadvantage
1	I can eat in the fresh air.	There might be insects.
2	The food is better than the food I cook.	It's expensive.
3	Sandwiches are cheap and easy to prepare.	It might rain.
4	I can cook what I like.	I have to wash up afterwards.
5	I can try new and unusual food.	I might not like the food.
6	I can relax in my own kitchen.	I have to go shopping first.

A restaurant **B** picnic **C** at home

7 ▶ 09 Listen to two candidates doing the exam task in Activity 6. Tick (✓) the advantages and disadvantages they mention.

8 Listen again. Which phrases do the candidates use to agree, disagree and explain? Tick (✓) the ones you hear.

agree	disagree	explain
Me too.	I can't agree.	That's because …
I agree.	I don't agree.	The reason is …
I think the same.	I don't like … at all.	That's why …

Reading

Multiple choice (Part 4) ▶ CB page 16

About the exam:

In this part of the exam you read a text and answer five multiple-choice questions. There are four options to choose from. One question may ask about the writer's feelings about something.

Strategy:

- Look at the questions quickly.
- Read the whole text.
- Read the questions carefully. Questions 1 and 5 are about the whole text.
- Identify the parts of the text where you can find the answers to the other questions.
- Check every option carefully, then choose the one that answers the question.

1 **Put the words in the correct order to make sentences about food.**

1 I / like / wouldn't / eat / to / meal / that / like / a

2 food / enough / isn't / there / plate / on / the

3 good / should / food / look / on / nice / plate / the

2 **Read the text and questions. For each question, mark the correct letter A, B, C or D.**

Every time I open a newspaper there's another article about changing the way we eat. First we were told it should be the Mediterranean **diet**, with its **emphasis** on tomatoes , olive oil and fish. I love all these foods so I really thought the Mediterranean diet was the one for me. Then I read that the Japanese diet would be even better, especially if I wanted to lose weight. Rice, seaweed, soya bean products and fish are the key **ingredients** here. I think sushi is delicious so the Japanese diet sounded like a good idea.

Then I read an article about something called the Caveman diet. This time it's meat that is the most important food but our **ancestors** also ate eggs, fish and seafood. They enjoyed eating fruit and vegetables too, so that's good news. The trouble is, if I decide to eat like a cavewoman, I'll have to give up all **processed** foods like chocolate and crisps. And I love chocolate and crisps!

Mediterranean, Japanese or Caveman? They all sound healthy, **nutritious** and quite tasty but what really matters is variety. I think we should have a little of all the things we love.

1 What is the writer doing in the text?

A recommending a way to lose weight

B giving her opinion about what we should eat

C complaining that newspapers tell us how to eat

D explaining why she doesn't like some foods

2 What can a reader find out from this text?

A Traditional diets are often recommended.

B Traditional diets are not very good for most people.

C Traditional diets have nothing in common with each other.

D Traditional diets are not very varied in their food.

3 Why doesn't the writer follow the Mediterranean diet?

A She doesn't like olive oil.

B She doesn't think it's very healthy.

C She discovered some other diets.

D She likes chocolate and crisps.

4 What does the writer say about the Caveman diet?

A She thinks it has too much meat.

B She would find it difficult to follow.

C She is going to try it.

D She feels it has too little fruit.

5 What would be the best title for this text?

A Eat what you enjoy

B Eat for health

C Eat a traditional diet

D Eat like your ancestors

3 **Complete the sentences with a word in bold from the text in Activity 2.**

1 Some of my .... left Ireland in the 1870s because they couldn't get enough to eat.

2 Doctors put a lot of .... on eating healthy food.

3 I'll have to go on a .... I'm really putting on weight!

4 I was going to make sushi but I don't have all the ....

5 Soya bean products are supposed to be very ....

6 .... foods often have a lot of artificial colouring.

4 **Match questions 1–4 with answers A–D.**

1 Do you often go on a diet?

2 Do you like food advertisements?

3 Do you buy food because it is cheap?

4 What's your favourite food?

A Not much, because they make food look better than it is.

B No, because it may not be good quality.

C Fruit, because it's good for me!

D No, because I never put on weight.

Vocabulary

suffixes ▶ CB page 17

1 Add a suffix from the box to the words in brackets to complete the sentences.

-able	-ful	-less	-ment

1 I won't buy tablecloths unless they're .... (*wash*). Dry-cleaning is so expensive!

2 I love the .... (*advertise*) for food on television. They're so funny!

3 I'm very .... (*care*) when I cook – I always make a big mess in the kitchen!

4 Eating in a restaurant can be very .... (*enjoy*) if the food is good.

5 I'm trying to put less sugar in my coffee; now I only have one .... (*spoon*) instead of three!

6 I'm a terrible cook but I'm .... (*hope*) that I will get better with practice.

7 I try to measure ingredients when I cook – you need to be .... (*care*) if you want it to taste good.

8 He's a .... (*hope*) cook! I can't eat his food!

2 Find and correct the mistakes with suffixes in the sentences.

1 I only wear clothes that are washful when I cook.

2 I'm very careless when I cook. I always make sure everything is exactly right.

3 I love cakes. I often buy an armless from the local shop!

4 I think that people get a lot of enjoyable from good food.

5 I love cooking. I find it very enjoyment.

Grammar

present simple and continuous
▶ CB page 18

1 Find and correct the mistakes with verb forms in the sentences. There are mistakes in five of the sentences. Tick (✓) the sentence that is correct.

1 I'm not really enjoying watching cooking programmes on TV. I think they're boring.

2 Can you answer the phone? I cook and my hands are covered in oil.

3 First you fry the onions. Then you add the spices.

4 This pineapple is weighing almost a kilo. It's enormous!

5 I try to find a recipe for tiramisu on the internet but there are so many I don't know where to start.

6 I'm not knowing how to make a Spanish omelette.

2 Read the email to decide if this sentence is correct or incorrect.

Sara always has a really big breakfast.

Hi Nick,

How are you? It's the Easter holidays here and I **(1)** .... (*enjoy*) just staying at home. It's always the same in the holidays – I never **(2)** .... (*get up*) early and I always **(3)** .... (*spend*) ages having breakfast. Normally, I **(4)** .... (*not have*) time for more than a bowl of cereal and a cup of tea so it's a real treat. Of course, at the weekends Josh sometimes **(5)** .... (*cook*) a traditional English breakfast. **(6)** .... (*you/know*) how to do that? You **(7)** .... (*fry*) eggs, bacon, sausages, mushrooms and tomatoes and **(8)** .... (*make*) loads of toast to go with it.

Josh and I **(9)** .... (*try*) to lose weight at the moment but it's very hard at Easter. We **(10)** .... (*only/have*) fruit and yoghurt this week to prepare for the proper diet. Every year I **(11)** .... (*promise*) myself I won't eat too many Easter eggs but I'm a chocoholic, as you **(12)** .... (*know*), and they are so delicious!

Anyway, I have to go now. Write soon and tell me about your Easter holidays.

Love,

Sara

3 Complete the email in Activity 2 with the present simple or present continuous form of the verbs in brackets.

4 Look at these groups of sentences. Find the one sentence in each group where the adverb of frequency or time expression is in the wrong position.

1 A I sometimes only have a cup of coffee for breakfast.
  B Sometimes I only have a cup of coffee for breakfast.
  C I only have sometimes a cup of coffee for breakfast.

2 A I'm learning how to cook Thai food at the moment.
  B I'm at the moment learning how to cook Thai food.
  C At the moment I'm learning how to cook Thai food.

3 A Do you usually cook your own meals?
  B Do you cook your own meals usually?
  C Do you cook usually your own meals?

4 A I don't during the week have much time for lunch.
  B I don't have much time for lunch during the week.
  C During the week I don't have much time for lunch.

Listening
Multiple choice (Part 2) ▶ CB page 19

1 ▶ 10 **You will hear an interview with a young man called Chris Jones, who works as a presenter and chef on a television cookery show. For each question, mark the correct letter, A, B or C.**

1 Why did Chris decide to become a chef?
   A His family encouraged him.
   B His friends shared his interest.
   C His teachers said he had talent.

2 Chris opened his own restaurant because
   A he liked the idea of working for himself.
   B he wanted to cook his own dishes.
   C he hoped to make money.

3 Chris's favourite food is fish because
   A it is healthy.
   B he can cook it in different ways.
   C it's different from food he ate as a child.

4 How does Chris feel about working on a television series?
   A He is happy to be famous.
   B He is pleased to be working with other chefs.
   C He is surprised to have got the opportunity.

5 Before the first television programme, Chris felt
   A worried about cooking bad food.
   B embarrassed about making a mistake.
   C afraid of forgetting something.

6 What does Chris say is most important to him for the future?
   A opening more restaurants
   B travelling to other countries
   C writing a book

2 Match verbs 1–5 to phrases A–E to make collocations.

1 shop   A the quality of food
2 find   B products to a person's home
3 see   C online
4 scan   D special deals
5 deliver   E a product at the supermarket

3 Complete the sentences with collocations from Activity 2 in the correct form. Make any changes necessary.

1 I think you get a better deal by _____ instead of going to a supermarket yourself.
2 At the supermarket the assistant _____ you want to buy at the checkout.
3 I always _____ by looking at advertisements in the newspaper – you can save money!
4 I always check fruit before I buy it – it's important to _____ so that you don't buy anything bad.

Grammar
modals of possibility ▶ CB page 20

1 Complete the sentences with *must*, *might* or *can't* and the verbs in brackets.

1 That _____ (be) an apple – it's the wrong shape. It _____ (be) a banana.
2 It _____ (rain) tonight so maybe we'd better take a taxi to the restaurant.
3 You _____ (be) hungry. You haven't had anything to eat all day.
4 This _____ (be) the right restaurant. Joe said it served Indian food and this is Italian.
5 I think I _____ (eat) chicken tonight – I had fish last night.
6 This _____ (have) garlic in it – I can taste it.

2 Find and correct the mistakes in the sentences.

1 He must be a vegetarian because I saw him eating a steak last night.
2 It can't be time to leave the restaurant. It's after midnight and we're the only people here!
3 That might be a strawberry. It's the right shape, size and colour so there's nothing else it can be.
4 I can't decide what to eat. I must have fish or I must have chicken – they both look good.
5 It's good to eat local food when you travel, though sometimes it must not be something you like!
6 This might not be the price! It's far too expensive!

Writing
Story (Part 3) ▶ CB page 21

1 Match questions 1–3 with answers A–C.

1 How often do you eat out?
2 What sort of restaurant do you prefer?
3 What kind of food do you recommend?

A Not expensive ones. But I enjoy pizza!
B Anything that's healthy!
C About once a week, usually at weekends.

2 Put the sentences in the correct order to make a story.

A I went to answer it.
B When my parents came home, they had no idea anything had happened.
C He had gone to get a glass of water and seen that the oven was on fire.
D My parents were out and I put spaghetti on for dinner.
E My brother started shouting from the kitchen.
F We put the fire out.
G The phone rang.

3 Read the full story and choose the correct alternatives.

A COOKING DISASTER

My parents were out and I decided to make spaghetti for dinner. I put some water on to boil but, unfortunately, I turned on the wrong burner. (1) *Eventually / Just then*, the phone rang. I left the cloth I had been using on top of the cooker and went to answer it. I must have been talking for quite a while when, (2) *suddenly / finally*, I heard my brother shouting from the kitchen. (3) *A few moments earlier / Finally*, he had gone to get a glass of water and seen that the cloth was on fire. Luckily, we managed to put the fire out but there was a lot of smoke. (4) *Eventually / Suddenly*, we got rid of it by opening all the windows. When my parents came home, they had no idea anything had happened.

4 Look at the exam task and the notes a candidate has written. Put the notes in the correct order.

> Your English teacher has asked you to write a story. Your story must begin with this sentence.
> *It was one of the worst experiences I have ever had in a restaurant.*

A didn't have enough money to pay bill
B invited my friend to have dinner for her birthday
C only had £5 in my pocket
D she ordered the most expensive things on menu
E realised I didn't have my wallet
F wanted to impress her so told her to order anything she wanted
G friend had credit card so she paid
H got home and found my wallet on bed
I waiter brought bill – £50!!

5 Use the notes in Activity 4 to write the story.

Mind your manners

Speaking

Extended turn (Part 3) ▶ CB page 24

1 Look at the photo below and decide if the sentences are true or false.

1 The people are waiting to pay in a supermarket.
2 They are all wearing winter clothes.
3 They are carrying shopping bags.
4 There are a lot of shelves with food on.
5 The people have been waiting a long time because they look annoyed.

2 Read what a candidate said about the photo in Activity 1. Complete the text with the words in the box.

---
angry   casual   queue   shelves   shopping baskets   suit
supermarket

I can see five people standing in a long **(1)** .... They are in a **(2)** .... because they have all been shopping and there are lots of **(3)** .... with food on. They are all carrying **(4)** .... with things in that they want to buy, and they have to pay the cashier. I think they have been waiting a long time because they look a little bit **(5)** ....! All the people are wearing **(6)** .... summer clothes except the last man, who is wearing a smart **(7)** .... He must be on his way home from work.

3 ▶ 11 Listen and check your answers to Activity 2.

General conversation (Part 4) ▶ CB page 24

4 When you discuss things, there are useful phrases and expressions for keeping the conversation going. Match discussion phrases 1–5 with responses A–E.

1 Sorry, can I say something?
2 Do you agree?
3 Sorry, could you say that again?
4 I don't get what you mean.
5 So what you mean is it's too cold to go.

A No, I'm sorry, I don't. I have to disagree with you.
B What I said was I don't know the answer.
C Of course, go ahead.
D Yes, that's exactly what I mean.
E Well, what I mean is, I think it's a good idea.

5 Two candidates are talking about times when they don't mind queuing and times when they hate it. Complete their conversation with phrases from Activity 4.

A: I hate waiting in queues when I'm in a hurry – you know, like when I've got up late or something and I have to wait in a queue to buy a ticket.
(1) ....?

B: Yes, I do! And I hate queuing when someone at the front is taking a long time and doesn't seem to understand that there are other people waiting.

A: Sorry, **(2)** ....

B: Well, what I mean is, they have no awareness of other people – they are just selfish.

A: But maybe they have a difficult problem. What I hate is when there are not enough people dealing with customers – you know, not enough checkouts open – that sort of thing.

B: Sorry, **(3)** ....?

A: Not enough checkouts open – that sort of thing.

B: So **(4)** .... there should be more checkouts, that it's the shop's fault that there is a queue.

A: Exactly! I don't mind queuing when I have someone to talk to or when I have plenty of time, or when …

B: Sorry, can I say something?

A: Sure, **(5)** ....

B: OK … I don't mind queuing when I know there's a good reason. I hate it when I'm in a traffic jam though.

A: I agree!

6 ▶ 12 **Listen and check your answers to Activity 5.**

7 **Match the speakers from Activities 5 and 6 with the questions. Write** *M* **(Man),** *W* **(Woman) or** *B* **(Both) next to each question.**

Who hates queuing when

1 they don't have much time? ....
2 other people take a long time? ....
3 there are not enough people working to help people in the queue? ....
4 there is a lot of traffic? ....

Vocabulary

phrasal verbs ▶ CB page 25

1 **Replace the underlined words in the sentences with a phrasal verb in the correct form. You may need to make changes to other words in the sentence.**

1 I don't know what this word means – I must <u>check it</u> in the dictionary.
2 I hate it when people <u>play their music very loud</u> when they're listening to it on the train.
3 I <u>have a very good relationship</u> with my sister.
4 I refuse to wait if I'm in a queue for anything – I just <u>stop waiting</u> and go home.
5 I love <u>taking care of</u> my neighbour's children – we have such fun together.
6 I never mind what people think about me. I just <u>continue</u> behaving in the same way.
7 Come on – we're late! Please <u>get moving</u>!
8 I hate <u>tidying</u> my bedroom. I have so much stuff in it!
9 I must finish my homework soon. I've got to <u>give it to the teacher</u> tomorrow morning.
10 I love <u>spending time</u> with my friends at the weekend.

describing feelings ▶ CB page 26

2 **Complete the sentences with the words in the box.**

amused	annoyed	confident	embarrassed
excited	nervous	satisfied	surprised

1 We were all really .... by his jokes – he made us laugh.
2 I feel quite .... when I have to meet new people – it's quite scary.
3 I get very .... when people use mobile phones on the train – it's incredibly rude.
4 I love birthdays – I get very .... about getting lots of presents!
5 I get .... when people thank me – I never know what to say and I often go red.
6 I feel very .... when something I do goes well – it makes me feel good.
7 When I play tennis, I'm always .... that I can win – I play very well.
8 I am often .... by things I read in the newspapers – I definitely don't believe everything!

Listening

True/False (Part 4) ▶ CB page 26

1 ▶ **13 You will hear two friends, Carol and Peter, talking about choosing food in a restaurant. Listen and decide if each sentence is correct or incorrect. If it is correct, put a tick (✓) in the box under A for YES. If it is incorrect, put a tick (✓) in the box under B for NO.**

		A	B
1	Peter really liked the restaurant when he visited it before.	☐	☐
2	Carol is sorry that she doesn't have much time.	☐	☐
3	Peter made a mistake with the time of the meeting.	☐	☐
4	Carol enjoys cooking at home.	☐	☐
5	Peter thinks that salad is a boring thing to eat.	☐	☐
6	Carol agrees with what Peter says about olive oil.	☐	☐

2 Listen again and write the phrases the speakers use to agree or disagree. Then decide if each phrase is used to agree or disagree.

1 **Carol:** I'm not fond of cooking.

   Peter: ....

             (agree / disagree)

2 **Peter:** I know it'll be nice and healthy.

   Carol: ....

             (agree / disagree)

3 **Peter:** You should try different dressings, like olive oil. They make all the difference.

   Carol: ....

             (agree / disagree)

Grammar

-ing forms and infinitives ▶ CB page 27

1 What is a friend? Choose the correct alternative in each sentence.

A friend is someone who

1 always supports you without *to ask / asking* questions.

2 wants *to show / showing* you kindness and respect.

3 enjoys *to spend / spending* time with you.

4 is happy *to tell / telling* you the truth at all times.

5 keeps *to make / making* you laugh.

6 decides *to stay / staying* with you when times are difficult.

7 accepts who you are without *to try / trying* to change you.

8 dislikes *to hurt / hurting* you.

2 Write the verbs in the box in the correct column to complete the table.

| arrange | can't stand | can't wait | expect |
| involve | learn | mind | practise |

verb + *-ing* form	verb + infinitive
....	....
....	....
....	....
....	....

3 Find and correct the mistakes in the text. There are six mistakes.

Friendship

- Friends are an important part of most people's lives. According to research, to have quality relationships means that you feel happier.

- If it's difficult seeing your friends every day or if you can't wait meeting them, you can always arrange keeping in touch online.

- Friends choose loving you for who you are, not what you look like — it's what's on the inside that they are interested in. To keep a friendship going, you have to decide doing as much as you can for them too — friendship is a two-way street!

Reading

True/False (Part 3) ▶ CB page 28

1 Look at the sentences about what a writer says about good manners on social networking sites. Read the text to decide if each sentence is correct or incorrect. If it is correct, mark it A. If it is incorrect, mark it B.

		A	B
1	Most people are naturally well-mannered.	☐	☐
2	Because social networking is quite new, we need advice on good manners for these sites.	☐	☐
3	Posting a comment on a friend's wall is OK as long as you are not rude about them.	☐	☐
4	If you invite all your friends to an event, they might think you don't really care if they can come or not.	☐	☐
5	There might be a problem if you tag your friend in a photo without asking them first.	☐	☐
6	Having a lot of friends on a social networking site doesn't necessarily mean that you are very popular.	☐	☐
7	Unfriending is not the best way of dealing with people you don't know or don't like.	☐	☐
8	If social networking becomes a substitute for real friendships, you have a problem.	☐	☐
9	You don't need to tell people that you are closing your account.	☐	☐
10	You should give everyone your email address or phone number if you close your account.	☐	☐

VIRTUAL GOOD MANNERS

You might not think so but most of us are actually quite **polite**. We thank people for gifts, for help or for just being kind to us and we apologise if we hurt them, damage their **belongings** or offend them, even very slightly. Most of this is second nature to us. We don't even have to think about it. But we do have to think quite carefully about how to be polite on social networking sites simply because they haven't **been around** for long. Here is some advice that might help you to be a well-mannered social networker.

● Don't comment. Send a message.
If you don't want everyone to see a comment, send a message instead of posting on the person's wall or commenting on their wall posts. This is especially important if the comment might offend other people or if it involves something your friend wouldn't want everyone to see.

● Don't invite all your friends to events.
Is it really possible for your friend to attend the event? If they live too far away or you know it's not their **thing**, then don't invite them. It shows that you are a person who is aware of your friends' individual **circumstances**.

● Don't tag your friends in photos without their permission.
You might think everyone will enjoy seeing you and your friends partying on the beach in Ibiza but your friend's mother might not be so **impressed**. Tagging someone in a photo can have serious **consequences** so check that your friend is happy about it before you tag them.

● Don't accept every friend invitation.
It's **flattering** to think that lots of people want to be our friends but are all the people on your friends list really friends? If your answer is 'no', then unfriending the people you don't actually know or like is something to consider. A much better and more polite approach is to think before you accept friend requests. Don't accept requests from people you don't know or don't particularly like. That way you don't have to hurt their feelings later on by unfriending them.

● What if it all gets too much?
Sometimes social networking just becomes too much. You realise that you're spending more time on social networking than you are with your real friends. That's the time to think about closing your account. If you do, make sure you warn your friends first, otherwise they might think you've simply deleted them from your friends list. You don't have to explain yourself. Just say goodbye and tell your real friends that they can use other methods to contact you if they need to.

2 Complete the sentences with a word in bold from the text on page 21. In one of the sentences you have to change the form of the word.

1 Tom is a very .... young man. He always sends a thank-you letter if you give him a gift.

2 If you don't start studying for the exams soon, you'll just have to face the ....

3 I wasn't .... at all when Alex told me he had a Ferrari.

4 Luxury cars are just not my ....

5 Are there any .... in which you would consider stealing?

6 When I was at school, I was always losing my ....

7 I was very .... when Tina told me she thought I was one of the cleverest people she had ever met.

8 Smart phones have .... for quite a few years now.

Vocabulary

phrasal verbs ▶ CB page 28

1 Match the first half of the definitions (1–6) with the second (A–F).

1 You ring someone up

2 You hang up

3 You ring someone back

4 You switch your mobile off

5 You carry on

6 You turn your mobile on

A when you've finished talking or if you get very angry.

B if you want to talk to them.

C a conversation or a phone call.

D when you're not allowed to use it or if you don't want to be interrupted.

E when it's OK to use it and you want to make and receive calls.

F if you couldn't talk to them earlier or if you didn't finish your conversation.

Grammar

modals of obligation ▶ CB page 30

1 Complete this conversation between two friends with the correct form of *have to*, *must* or *should*.

A: Are you going to that speed dating event on Saturday?

B: I can't go this weekend after all but I want to go the following weekend. I **(1)** .... remember to tell them I want to change the day.

A: Can you do that?

B: Yes, basically. But you **(2)** .... tell them four days in advance and you also **(3)** .... pay €5 extra.

A: Perhaps I could go this weekend in your place.

B: No, I'm afraid that's not possible. You **(4)** .... be registered with FastDate and you're not a girl!

A: Oh! So if someone takes your place, they **(5)** .... be the same sex as you? Tell me more about it. **(6)** .... (*you*) wear special clothes?

B: No, but everyone wants to make a good impression so you **(7)** .... try and look your best. I usually wear jeans and a smart jacket.

A: How long do you get to talk to each person?

B: Five minutes. Then a bell rings and you **(8)** .... move to the next table. That should be enough time to decide if you might want to see that person again.

A: What happens if you run out of things to say?

B: Well, it's a good idea to prepare some questions in advance, just in case, but not too many – you **(9)** .... try to be natural and spontaneous.

A: If you like someone, what **(10)** .... (*you*) do next?

B: After each conversation you put a tick next to the person's name if you want to see them again. I think you **(11)** .... try and make a few notes as well to help you remember the person. Then, the next day, you **(12)** .... go to the FastDate website and enter your ticks online. If the other person has ticked you too, you get each other's contact details so you can arrange a date.

A: It sounds great! You **(13)** .... forget to email me the website address so I can register too.

2 ▶ 14 Listen and check your answers to Activity 1.

Writing

Message (Part 2) ▶ CB page 31

About the exam:

In this part of the exam you write a short message in 35–45 words. This can be an email, a note or a postcard.

Strategy:

- The task tells you who to write to and the kind of message you need to write.
- There are three bullet points: these tell you the sort of information you need to write.
- Write the message in full sentences.
- Check what you have written to make sure spelling, punctuation and grammar are correct.
- Check that you have included all the information from the bullet points.

1 Look at the exam task and decide if the sentences that follow it are true or false.

> An English girl called Lucy that you met at a speed dating event has sent you an email to say she would like to see you again. Write a reply email to Lucy. In your email you should:
>
> - say you were pleased to receive her message.
> - say what you liked about her when you spoke to her at the event.
> - suggest when and where you could meet again.
>
> Write 35–45 words.

1 In her message Lucy probably said something like, 'You seem like a really fun person. I really enjoyed talking to you. Shall we meet up some time?'

2 You can say that you don't want to meet up with her.

3 You need to think of something nice to say about Lucy.

4 You should think of a day or time to meet.

5 You have to suggest a place to meet.

6 You must write exactly 45 words.

2 Look at the emails two candidates wrote for the exam task in Activity 1. Which candidate, Kristian or Stefan, wrote the friendliest message?

> Hi Lucy,
>
> I liked your message. I thought you were very pretty and intelligent. we can meet next saturday. Club Seven is good. See you there at eight o'clock.
>
> Stefan

> Hi Lucy,
>
> It was great to get your message. I thought you were really good fun too. That joke you told me was hilarious? How about meeting up next Saturday? We could go to a movie and then get something to eat. what do you think?
>
> Kristian

3 Find and correct the mistakes in the emails in Activity 2. There are two mistakes in each email.

4 Now write your answer to this exam task.

> Pamela, a friend of yours from a social networking site, has sent you an invitation to an English conversation evening she is having at her home next Saturday. Send a reply email to Pamela. In your email you should:
>
> - thank her for her invitation.
> - explain that you might arrive a bit late.
> - offer to bring something to eat or drink.
>
> Write 35–45 words.

Leaving a record

Reading

Multiple-choice cloze (Part 5)   ▶ CB page 32

About the exam:
In this part of the exam you read a text with ten words missing. There are four options for each missing word. You choose the option which fits best in the space. The options test vocabulary and words with similar meanings, and also grammatical points such as pronouns, modals, prepositions and linking words.

Strategy:
- Read the title and the whole text to see what it is about.
- Read the text again carefully and think about the missing words. You may know what the answer is!
- Look at the four options and choose the best one for each space.

1 Choose six words from the box to describe the photo.

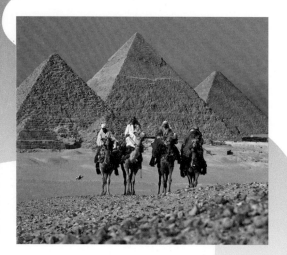

camels   countryside   desert   dry   hot   mountains   pyramid   sandy

2 Complete the sentences with your own ideas.

1 The most interesting place I've ever visited was .... because ....

2 A place I would like to visit in the future is .... because ....

3 Match these famous archaeological sites (1–5) with the texts (A–E).

1 Machu Picchu, Peru

2 Stonehenge, England

3 Pompeii, Italy

4 Moai Statues of Easter Island, Chile

5 Nazca Lines, Peru

A These massive statues were carved between AD1400 and 1600 out of compressed volcanic ash. Many are still standing in different places around the island.

B These giant drawings in the Peruvian desert show humans and animals. They can be seen clearly from the sky but not from the ground.

C When Mount Vesuvius erupted in AD79, thousands died but the ash preserved the bodies and the buildings. Archaeologists can study what daily life was like in the Italian city.

D The whole site was constructed over thousands of years, although no one knows what it was for or how it was built. The stones are instantly recognisable by visitors to the UK.

E It was built high in the Andes mountains by the Inca in the fifteenth century, though no one knows why. It is now one of the New Seven Wonders of the World.

4 Read the article and choose the correct word(s) for each space. For each question, mark the correct letter A, B, C or D.

AN UNEXPECTED RESULT OF SPACE EXPLORATION

Space exploration has changed our lives. It has given us many new products and changed the **(0)** _A way_ we live, communicate and travel. The business world has benefitted **(1)** .... – just think about the number of new jobs that there are, **(2)** .... advances in technology.

(3) ...., there is one way in which technology has had surprising results: it has improved our knowledge of history! It seems strange that something changing our lives **(4)** .... the future can also help us understand the past. This is **(5)** .... it happens: satellites that are orbiting the planet **(6)** .... back photographs of the surface of the Earth. These **(7)** .... sites of ancient civilisations, places **(8)** .... cities have been buried over the centuries. These sites can't be seen from the ground because they are buried so **(9)** .... in the earth. 'Space archaeology' can find these sites but then scientists and archaeologists have to depend **(10)** .... traditional methods of digging to explore them!

0	**A** way	**B** method	**C** type	**D** life
1	**A** in addition	**B** as well	**C** along with	**D** on top of
2	**A** due to	**B** because	**C** as	**D** so as
3	**A** But	**B** So	**C** Also	**D** However
4	**A** in	**B** at	**C** by	**D** with
5	**A** how	**B** who	**C** that	**D** what
6	**A** direct	**B** post	**C** send	**D** push
7	**A** see	**B** seem	**C** look	**D** show
8	**A** which	**B** where	**C** what	**D** why
9	**A** low	**B** down	**C** deep	**D** small
10	**A** for	**B** of	**C** on	**D** off

5 Find words in the article in Activity 4 to match definitions 1–4.

1 got an advantage from
2 made better than before
3 going round (the Earth)
4 put under the ground

Vocabulary

linking words: addition and contrast
▶ CB page 33

1 Choose the correct alternative in each sentence.

1 *Although / However* I am not interested in history, I like watching historical films.
2 I love going to museums *as well as / too* art galleries.
3 I'd love to go to Egypt *although / even* it's very hot in the summer.
4 I learn about history from books and *also / so* from the internet.
5 I haven't read a history book in years *in spite of / although* the fact that I studied it at school.
6 *Despite / Though* the rain, we still went to the museum.
7 My brother hates visiting museums. He came with us *despite / though*.
8 We visited a number of historical sites and quite a few museums *as well as / too*.

2 Complete the sentences with linking words from Activity 1.

1 I love visiting old buildings .... the fact that some of them are not very well kept.
2 My best friend enjoys visiting old places .... going on beach holidays.
3 .... the high cost, we decided to buy tickets to the exhibition.
4 I don't like spending time on the internet .... I can find lots of information there.
5 I really enjoy reading history books. ...., my friend doesn't. I'm not really interested in watching historical films .... – they seem so unreal.
6 He loves watching historical films. He .... enjoys visiting museums and historical sites.

Grammar

present perfect and past simple
▶ CB page 34

1 **Complete the sentences with *for* or *since*.**

1 I've known my closest friend .... about ten years.

2 I've been a student here .... three weeks.

3 I've had my mobile phone .... February.

4 My friend has had the same hairstyle .... he was 14.

5 I've liked my favourite singer .... a really long time.

6 We've lived in our house .... 2002.

2 **Make questions with *How long …?* to which the sentences in Activity 1 are the answers.**

3 **Answer the questions in Activity 2 about yourself.**

4 **Complete the sentences with the past simple or present perfect form of the verbs in brackets.**

A It's great but I'm thinking about getting a different one that .... (*come out*) last month.

B I ....(*not make*) many new friends yet.

C He thinks it's time for a change though so he ....(*decide*) to let it grow. Finally!

D A couple of months ago I .... (*see*) her play in London.

E My parents ....(*buy*) it after we ....(*move*) here from Buenos Aires.

F We ....(*do*) so many different things together.

5 **Match the sentences in Activity 1 with the sentences in Activity 4.**

Speaking

Simulated situation (Part 2) ▶ CB page 35

About the exam:
In this part of the exam you and the other candidate speak to each other. The examiner doesn't speak. The examiner gives you and the other candidate a situation to discuss. There are some pictures to help you in your discussion but you can also use your own ideas.

Strategy:
• Listen to the other candidate and make comments and suggestions.
• Talk for as long as you can about all the ideas in the pictures.
• Don't hurry to reach a conclusion.

1 ▶ 15 **Look at the exam task and then listen to a conversation between two candidates. Which objects from the picture do they decide not to put in the time capsule?**

In the next part you are going to talk to each other. I'm going to describe a situation to you. You have decided to make a time capsule so that people who live a hundred years from now can learn about life today. Talk together about the things you could put in the time capsule and decide which two things would give a clear picture of the way we live now.

2 **Complete these sentences from the conversation in Activity 1.**

1 Do you .... we should choose small things?

2 How .... the mobile phone?

3 We .... put lots of different kinds of music on it.

4 .... do you think about the money?

5 .... we could just use the front page.

6 So .... put the fashion magazine, the money, the front page of the newspaper and the recipe in our capsule.

3 **Listen again and check your answers to Activity 2.**

Listening

Multiple choice (Part 1) ▶ CB page 36

1 ▶ 16 **Listen to the recording and write the words in the box in the correct column to complete the table.**

artist   catalogue   exhibit   guide   history
painting   sculpture   shop

1 **O**	
2 **Oo**	
3 **Ooo**	
4 **oOo**	

2 ▶ 17 **Listen to the recording. For each question, choose the correct picture and put a tick (✓) in the box below it.**

1 Where is the art gallery?

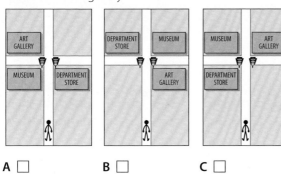

A ☐   B ☐   C ☐

2 What did the woman like best in the museum?

A ☐   B ☐   C ☐

3 When is the best day for students to visit the museum?

A ☐   B ☐   C ☐

4 What did the man buy in the museum shop?

A ☐   B ☐   C ☐

5 What does the girl say is most useful to her?

A ☐   B ☐   C ☐

6 What has the boy kept the longest?

A ☐   B ☐   C ☐

7 Where does the woman want to go at the weekend?

A ☐   B ☐   C ☐

4

Grammar

used to ▶ CB page 37

1 Complete the sentences with *used to* and the verbs in the box.

go	have	live	make	see	tell

1 I .... in Melbourne.
2 I .... a next door neighbour called Diana.
3 We .... each other every day.
4 We .... to a café to have coffee and talk.
5 Diana .... very funny jokes.
6 She .... me laugh so much it hurt.

2 Put the words in the correct order to make a conversation.

1 in / winter / you / didn't / go / skiing / use / to / ?
2 Yes. / Switzerland / used / two / weeks / we / always / to go / for / to
3 use / did / go / to / in / always / you / January / ?
4 Yes. / same / used / see / the / people / to / we / always / there
5 what / most / did / you / use / enjoy / to / ?
6 Everything! / falling / over / only / was / thing / use / didn't / to / I / enjoy / the

3 Complete the sentences about the photographs with *used to* and a suitable verb.

1 A lot of people .... the train to work.
2 Most men .... hats.
3 Women .... trousers or jeans.

4 People only .... one TV, which they kept in the living room.
5 The whole family .... TV together.

Vocabulary

town and city ▶ CB page 38

1 Do the crossword.

Down: T O W N & C I T Y

1 typical weather conditions in an area
2 in a place near where you live
3 when something gets bigger or develops
4 adjective from 'friend'
5 services that are available in a place
6 a person who lives in a house very near you
7 films, shows, concerts, etc. that people like to watch
8 full of activity

2 Complete the blog with the words in the box. There are some words you do not need to use.

chances	facilities	fresh	friendly	going
growth	lively	local	mild	places
playgrounds	soft	spaces	transport	

▶ Santa Cruz de Tenerife, where I live, is one of the world's most liveable cities according to a recent article. The journalist commented on the **(1)** .... climate, excellent public **(2)** .... and the entertainment **(3)** .... There is a concert hall, a theatre, several museums and an art gallery. If you prefer to spend your time out in the **(4)** .... air, there are plenty of open **(5)** .... , even in the centre of the city, some of them with **(6)** .... for children. Though there has been quite rapid **(7)** .... over the last few years, you can still find **(8)** .... neighbours and a sense of community. My own neighbourhood is quite **(9)** .... There's always something **(10)** .... on and the **(11)** .... shops are great.

28

Writing

Sentence transformations (Part 1)

▶ CB page 39

About the exam:

In this part of the exam you rewrite five sentences, which are on the same topic. You are given a complete sentence and the beginning and end of a second, incomplete sentence. You rewrite the second sentence keeping the same meaning but using different words. You can only write up to three words.

Strategy:

- Read all the sentences to see what the topic is.
- Read each complete sentence first and think about its meaning.
- Decide what structure you need for the second sentence and think about any other changes you need to make.
- Complete the second sentence, then check your grammar, spelling and punctuation.

1 **Look at these groups of sentences. Find the one sentence in each group which has a completely different meaning.**

1 A The best way to learn the language is to live in the country.

B There is no better way to learn the language than living in the country.

C One way to learn the language is to live in the country.

2 A I love history although I don't study it seriously.

B I like history because I don't study it seriously.

C I enjoy history despite the fact that I don't study it seriously.

3 A I've just finished my work.

B I finished my work a short time ago.

C I finished my work some time ago.

4 A I could have studied harder.

B I should have studied harder.

C I ought to have studied harder.

5 A This is the best film I have ever seen.

B I liked this film less than any other.

C I have never seen a better film.

6 A I used to live in Italy.

B I lived in Italy before but not now.

C I am living in Italy.

2 **Complete the second sentence so that it means the same as the first. Use no more than three words.**

0 There is no better way of recording information than saving it onto a secure database.

The _____*best way to*_____ record information is saving it onto a secure database.

1 It is necessary for people to keep passwords safe.

People _____ keep passwords safe.

2 It is true that it can be difficult to remember some kinds of information, like passwords.

It is true that _____ some kinds of information, like passwords, can be difficult.

3 I had never forgotten my password before last week.

I _____ my password for the first time last week.

4 It was not as difficult as I had expected to set up a new password.

It was _____ than I had expected to set up a new password.

5 Some people worry too much about security.

Security is something that _____ some people too much.

3 **What grammar did you need to use in sentences 1–5 in Activity 2? Choose from the items in the box. There is one item you do not need to use.**

a comparative   an -ing form
a modal of obligation   a phrasal verb
past simple   present simple

Swap it

Vocabulary

clothes ▶ CB page 42

1 **Do the crossword.**

Across

2

6

7

8

Down

1

3

4

5

2 **Look at the photo. What are the people wearing?**

The girl on the right is wearing a shirt, jeans and boots.

3 **What's the difference? Complete the sentences with the pairs of words in the box.**

blouse/shirt	hat/cap	jacket/overcoat
shoes/boots	tie/scarf	trousers/jeans

1 Men wear a .... when they wear a suit but women wear a .... on top of a skirt.

2 Men wear a .... round their neck when they want to look smart but anyone wears a .... to keep their neck warm.

3 If it's cold, people wear an .... to go out but in the spring a .... is warm enough.

4 A .... keeps your head warm but a .... keeps the sun out of your eyes.

5 It's not a good idea to wear .... on your feet in the snow – you have to wear ....

6 It's very fashionable for men to wear .... instead of .... when they go out but it's not good to wear them to work because they're not smart enough.

4 **Match the first half of the compound adjectives (1–3) with the second (A–C).**

1 second-   **A** fashioned

2 old-   **B** date

3 up-to-   **C** hand

5 **Complete the sentences with the compound adjectives in Activity 4.**

1 The jeans I bought last year look really .... now. The styles have changed completely.

2 If you want to look ...., buy your clothes at Trendsetter Fashions.

3 You can get some really great .... stuff in that charity shop on the corner.

6 ▶ **18 You will hear a conversation between a man called Joe and his friend Helen about buying clothes. Listen and decide if the statements are true or false.**

1 Joe has to buy clothes for a special occasion.

2 Helen has a great interest in fashion.

3 Joe doesn't buy clothes very often.

4 Helen is not pleased that Joe doesn't like some colours.

5 Joe doesn't want to look old-fashioned.

6 Helen recommends buying clothes from a second-hand shop.

verbs related to clothes ▶ CB page 42

7 **Complete the sentences with the verbs in the box.**

borrow	fit	go with	iron	put on	suit
try on	wear out				

1 It's very important to .... clothes in the shop to check the size.

2 Some colours don't .... each other – like orange and red.

3 If clothes don't .... you because they are too big or too small, they look terrible.

4 I never buy clothes made of linen because I have to .... them after washing.

5 I get dressed very quickly in the mornings – it doesn't take me long to .... my clothes.

6 Children's clothes .... very quickly because they don't take care of them.

7 I hate all the clothes in the shops at the moment. These bright colours don't .... me at all.

8 My sister is always asking to .... my best leather jacket.

8 **Complete the second sentence so that it means the same as the first. Use no more than three words.**

1 I always make sure that my blouse is the same colour and style as my skirt.

I always make sure that my blouse .... with my skirt.

2 It's a good idea to wear clothes to check they're the right size before you buy them.

It's a good idea to .... clothes before you buy them.

3 It's difficult to decide what clothes to wear every morning, isn't it?

It's difficult to decide what clothes to .... on every morning, isn't it?

4 I can never throw away clothes when they get very old if I like them.

I can never throw away clothes when they wear .... if I like them.

5 It's difficult to get clothes that are the right size for me because I'm very tall.

It's difficult to get clothes to .... me because I'm very tall.

6 That blue shirt looks really good on you.

That blue shirt really .... you.

order of adjectives ▶ CB page 43

9 Choose the correct option to complete the sentence about the order of adjectives.

We put adjectives in the following order in sentences:

A opinion, size, colour, material

B size, opinion, material, colour

C colour, material, size, opinion

10 Find and correct the mistakes with the order of adjectives in the sentences.

1 I've just bought a beautiful silk blue dress but it was really expensive!

2 I love my cotton short skirt; it's great for hot weather.

3 My friend gave me a red horrible woollen sweater for my birthday!

4 I'm hoping to buy a cotton cheap blue dress to wear on the beach.

5 Max is wearing a velvet trendy red jacket – he looks very cool!

6 I'm going to the sales today. I want to buy a leather smart black jacket because my old one is worn out.

Speaking

Extended turn (Part 3) ▶ CB page 43

1 ▶ 19 Listen to a candidate describing one of the photos. Which one is he describing?

2 The second candidate is describing the other photo. Complete her turn. Use one word in each gap.

I can see two people shopping for clothes. They are talking and looking at the clothes in a shop. They can see some **(1)** .... hanging up and some **(2)** .... that are folded on a **(3)** .... I can see price tags but I don't know how much the clothes are. They are both wearing **(4)** .... clothes. One of the men is wearing a **(5)** .... jacket. They are interested in buying something new to wear.

3 ▶ 20 Now listen and check your answers.

General conversation (Part 4) ▶ CB page 43

4 ▶ 21 Listen to two candidates doing the exam task below and choose the correct option to answer the questions.

> I'd like you to talk about the kind of clothes you wear every day and the kind of clothes you wear when you go out.

1 What does the woman say about her clothes?

A She chooses them carefully.

B She wears the same things every day.

2 What does the man say about his everyday clothes?

A He doesn't have many different clothes.

B He tries to wear different things every day.

3 What does the woman say about going out?

A She worries about how she looks.

B She loves buying special clothes.

4 What does the man say about going out?

A He thinks clothes are not important.

B He wears smart clothes.

5 Listen again. What expressions do the candidates use to ask for each other's opinion? Tick (✓) the ones you hear.

1 Do you have any ideas?

2 What's your opinion?

3 How about you?

4 Do you think that's important?

5 Do you agree with me?

6 How do you feel about that?

7 What do you think?

8 And you?

9 Do you think I'm right?

10 What would you say?

Listening

Gap-fill (Part 3) ▶ CB page 44

About the exam:
In this part of the exam you hear one person giving information (e.g. to a group of people or speaking on the radio). You complete notes on what they say. You hear the recording twice.

Strategy:
- Read all the notes to get an idea of what the topic is.
- Try to guess what kind of word is missing: noun, verb, time, date, etc.
- The first time you listen fill in as much as you can.
- The second time check and complete all the answers.
- Make sure that your spelling is correct and that your writing is easy for the examiner to read.

1 You will hear a man talking about a club for pet lovers. Before you listen, read the leaflet and decide if the sentences are true or false.

1 The club is for people who already have a pet.

2 You have to pay to join the club.

Pet Share Club

Who can join the club?

You must be at least (1) .... to join.

What kind of pets are there?

The most popular pets are (2) ....

How does the club work?

- Most people rent a pet for a (3) ....

- It is better to make a booking in (4) .... because it's quicker.

- It's important to have a large (5) .... near your home.

What does it cost?

Annual membership costs (6) ....

2 Look at the leaflet in Activity 1 and try to guess what kind of word/information is missing in each gap.

3 ▶ 22 Listen and complete each gap in the leaflet in Activity 1 with one word from the recording.

Grammar

comparatives and superlatives
▶ CB page 45

1 Complete the sentences comparing pets with the correct form of the adjectives in brackets.

1 Cats are usually .... (*small*) dogs.
2 They are .... (*independent*) dogs.
3 Dogs are often .... (*noisy*) cats.
4 Tortoises are much .... (*easy*) to look after .... cats.
5 Cats are definitely .... (*affectionate*) tortoises.
6 Rabbits usually have .... (*soft*) fur .... dogs.

2 Some words are missing from this text. Complete it with the words in the box. Use one word for each sentence.

as	less	more	most	the	than

Dogs make best pets, in my opinion. They're much more fun cats, rabbits or tortoises. Tortoises have to be the boring pets in the world. My friend has a tortoise and he says they're interesting than I think. They're also a lot expensive to feed than other animals. They're not nearly friendly and affectionate though.

Reading

Matching (Part 2) ▶ CB page 46

1 The young people below are looking for somewhere to stay when they come to the UK. A candidate has underlined the important information in description 1. Underline the important information in descriptions 2–5.

1 Noelia <u>loves small children</u> and <u>enjoys cooking</u>. She is <u>studying architecture</u> and it is important for her to be able to <u>see famous buildings</u>. She <u>doesn't want to spend too much money</u>. ....

2 Piotr plays the drums. He would like to live with other students with similar interests. He loves animals and would like to have a pet. ....

3 Lakshmi is studying nursing. She wants to specialise in looking after old people. She loves classical music. She can have her meals at the hospital where she will be working. ....

4 Anneline needs to be near the university so she can study at weekends. She wants to make new friends while she is in the UK, especially people from other parts of the world. ....

5 Nourridine is studying to be a chef. He would like to be able to cook his own meals. He plans to bring his car to the UK. He would like to live with an English person. ....

2 Now read some advertisements for accommodation and underline the important information.

A We are a young couple with a baby, a cat and a lovely spare room in our flat. The room has wonderful views of many famous places in London, like Saint Paul's Cathedral. We offer a lower rent to someone who can prepare meals and help look after the baby at weekends.

B My husband and I live with our 14-year-old son, Simon, in a beautiful country house. Our other son is studying abroad and we would like to have a student to stay in his room, join us for family meals and also help Simon with his school work.

C There are still shared flats available in our International Student Lodge. You will have access to the library and car park at the university, which is across the road. Students from all over Europe, Asia, Africa and America have made Student Lodge their home. Why not join them?

D I am offering free accommodation in exchange for help with my mother, who is now almost 90. You will have your own room but I'm afraid I cannot provide meals or let you use the kitchen. I have a season ticket for the opera, which you are welcome to borrow from time to time.

E I'm looking for someone to share my flat with me. I'm a 22-year-old boy from Manchester. You will have your own room, use of the garage and access to the kitchen and laundry. No pets or smokers, I'm afraid.

F We have a room to rent in our house. There are three of us sharing. I'm from Sweden, Julio's from Argentina and Eddie, the dog, is from England! We are keen guitarists and we play together most evenings. I mean, Julio and I play; Eddie sometimes sings!

3 Now decide which kind of accommodation (A–F) would be the most suitable for each person (1–5).

Vocabulary
house and home ▶ CB page 47

1 Read the definitions. What are they describing?

1 It's the place you keep the car.
2 You hang them to cover windows.
3 You cover the floor with it.
4 It lets the smoke out of the house from the fireplace.
5 You turn it on in the summer to keep you cool at night.
6 You put it on your bed to keep you warm at night.

2 Choose the correct alternative in each sentence.

1 I appreciate old things – I always buy *antique / modern* furniture when I can afford it.
2 It's nice to have outdoor space – I eat breakfast on my *basement / balcony* every morning.
3 I love growing flowers but, unfortunately, my house doesn't have a *garden / drive*.
4 I live in a very hot country so it's important to have *central heating / air conditioning* in every house.
5 I have *blinds / glasses* on my windows for privacy.
6 I love having soft *cushions / pillows* on my bed – they help me sleep better.

Grammar
too and *enough*, *so* and *such* ▶ CB page 48

1 Rewrite the sentences with the words in brackets in the correct place.

1 Nicolas always wears smart clothes. (*such*)
2 Most performance cars are expensive for someone like me. (*too*)
3 There are only about 320,000 people in Iceland. I didn't know it was a small country. (*such*)
4 I'm not hungry to eat a whole pizza! (*enough*)
5 We were tired that we went straight to bed. (*so*)
6 There are not open spaces for children to play in my town. (*enough*)

2 Choose the correct alternative in each sentence.

1 It's *so / such* a cold day I think I'll turn the heating on.
2 It's *so / such* crowded on the bus in the evenings that I sometimes walk home instead.
3 There are *so / such* nice people in my class. I've made a lot of friends.
4 Ana is *so / such* friendly; she smiles and says hello to almost everyone she meets.
5 That's *so / such* a pretty dress! It really suits you.
6 Tina has *so / such* many friends! She's really popular.

Writing
Message (Part 2) ▶ CB page 49

1 Look at the exam task and the email a candidate has written. Underline the part of the task the candidate has not covered in his email.

You are going to live in the UK with a host family.
Write an email to a friend. In your email you should:
• say where you are going to live.
• say why you have decided to live there.
• invite your friend to visit you.
Write 35–45 words.

Hi Yiorgos,
Guess what? I'm going to live in London with a really nice host family. You can come and visit me if you like.
See you soon,
Jürgen

2 Write another sentence in your notebook to complete the email in Activity 1 so that it answers all the parts of the task.

3 Now look at this exam task and decide if the sentences are true or false.

You have decided to rent a pet for the weekend.
Write an email to a friend. In your email you should:
• say what kind of pet you are going to rent.
• say why you have decided to rent this particular kind of pet.
• invite your friend to come and meet the pet.

1 You can say that you are going to rent a dog or cat.
2 You must say how much it costs.
3 You should say why you like the kind of pet you have chosen.
4 You could say why you don't like other kinds of pets as much.
5 You must suggest that your friend comes to your house to see the pet.

4 Write your answer to the exam task in Activity 3.

Reading

Multiple choice (Part 4) ▶ CB page 50

1 **Read the article quickly and choose the best title for it.**

A You're never too old to learn
B I left it too late to learn
C Teach yourself to cycle

I'm 25 years old and I'm learning to ride a bicycle. You probably think that I have left it very late to start. In fact, I wouldn't be learning now if I hadn't been invited to go on a cycling holiday this summer. The idea of telling my friends that I couldn't ride a bike was too **embarrassing**. The time had come. I had to learn.

But why didn't my parents teach me when I was a child? Well, to begin with, we didn't have a bicycle. My parents always told us that my aunt, who had tried to learn to ride on her own, had fallen off and broken her arm. My grandparents were so **upset** that they decided to <u>give</u> the bicycle <u>away</u>. No one on my mother's side of the family had ridden a bicycle since then.

But now all that has changed. I started my lessons in the local park two months ago. My teacher **lowered** the seat of the bike so that I could put my

feet on the ground and I learnt to **balance** riding down gentle **grassy slopes**. When I fell off, it didn't hurt much at all. Now I can ride on hard surfaces and I love it.

If you're reading this and you didn't learn to ride a bike as a child, please believe that it is never too late. Find a class or get a friend to teach you. There's plenty of information on the internet about how to learn. If you fall off, <u>get up</u> and <u>get</u> back <u>on</u>. Don't <u>give up</u>. Cycling is great!

2 Read the article in Activity 1 again and the questions below. For each question, mark the correct letter, A, B, C or D.

1 What is the writer trying to do in the text?

A encourage others to learn to ride a bicycle

B explain why she didn't learn to ride a bicycle before

C criticise her parents for not teaching her to ride a bicycle

D describe a method for learning to ride a bicycle

2 The writer says she was too embarrassed

A to go on a cycling holiday with her friends.

B to start to learn to ride a bicycle.

C to tell her friends she didn't know how to ride a bicycle.

D to explain to people that she was learning to ride a bicycle.

3 The writer didn't ride a bicycle as a child because

A her parents gave the family bicycle away.

B she hurt herself when she was trying to learn.

C her parents didn't think it was a good idea.

D no one in her family had a bicycle.

4 The writer started learning to cycle in a park because

A it was near her house.

B she was too scared to cycle in the street.

C she was less likely to injure herself there.

D all the lessons were given there.

5 Which of these is closest in meaning to what the writer thinks about learning to cycle?

A Don't wait too long to start.

B It's much easier than I thought.

C You need a qualified teacher.

D Keep trying, no matter what.

3 Complete the definitions with a word in bold from the text in Activity 1.

1 pieces of ground that gradually get higher or lower: ....

2 unhappy because something unpleasant has happened: ....

3 stay in a steady position without falling to one side or the other: ....

4 covered with grass: ....

5 making you feel nervous or uncomfortable: ....

6 moved down: ....

4 Complete the sentences with an underlined phrasal verb from the article in Activity 1. You may need to change the form of some verbs.

1 My father is trying to .... smoking. He hasn't had a cigarette for two days now.

2 Don't just sit there! .... and do something!

3 I think I dropped my ticket as I was .... the train. I didn't have it when the conductor came round.

4 We've got four beautiful kittens to .... Please take one and give it a home!

Vocabulary

prepositional phrases ▶ CB page 51

1 Choose the correct alternatives to complete the article.

HOME | BLOG | WORLD SPORT FINANCE CULTURE TRAVEL
Politics | Obits | Education | Earth | Science | Defence | Health | Art

Why cartoons are not a waste of time

I learnt English in an unusual way. But for me, it worked! When I was little, we had satellite TV at home with an English language cartoon channel. My mum knew that English was an important language so even though I was only small, she made me watch it. **[1]** *At first / At all* the cartoons didn't mean much – **[2]** *at least / in fact*, I understood nothing – but **[3]** *at first / in the end*, as I started to understand the language and really enjoy the cartoons, I watched more and more.

So **[4]** *because of / at all* this, I picked up English in the same way as an English-speaking child – that is, through listening and experiencing it, and not learning it formally in a class. I couldn't analyse the grammar **[5]** *at all / in the end* so I couldn't explain it to anyone else but **[6]** *at least / at first* I used it naturally and instinctively.

When I did start learning English formally in school, I already knew most of it. But I still did the homework exercises because they were fun, and it was useful to keep my language **[7]** *in contact / up to date* and to correct any small mistakes I made. I plan to learn more languages, maybe in a similar way, although I know there are many good courses **[8]** *on sale / in fact* now. I'm sure the key to success in the modern world is being multilingual!

Grammar

past simple and past continuous ▶ CB page 52

1 **Match sentences 1–3 with uses A–C.**

1 I went to a fantastic college – the course was great and I made loads of friends.

2 While I was working on my project, my brother was studying for his English test.

3 I was studying in the library when my friend arrived.

A past continuous: two past actions in progress at the same time

B past continuous + past simple : a past action in progress when another action happened

C past simple: a completed past action

2 **Find and correct the mistakes in the sentences.**

1 I practised my English pronunciation when, suddenly, the telephone rang.

2 While I studied for my exam, my brother was playing football.

3 I was moving to Spain last year to learn Spanish.

4 My mother called me on my mobile while I spoke to my tutor.

5 I was passing my exam last week! I'm so happy!

6 I was watching television when my friend was calling me last night.

7 I was laughing when my friend told me the story!

8 I was taking a language course in England while my friend learnt French in France.

9 I saw my friend just as she walked past my window.

10 I knew the words but I wasn't understanding the grammar.

3 **Complete the email with the past simple or past continuous form of the verbs in the box.**

be   buy   cycle   discover   go   join   leave   meet
not know   rain   talk   worry

Hi Jack,

My first week at university is over. Things **(1)** .... really well! Before I **(2)** .... home, I **(3)** .... about feeling lonely but there **(4)** .... loads of things to do every day! I **(5)** .... loads of people at the welcome disco last Friday and while I **(6)** .... to one girl there called Jenny, I **(7)** .... that she attended the same primary school as me – although I **(8)** .... her then. Last Wednesday I **(9)** .... into town and **(10)** .... some clothes. It **(11)** .... and I got very wet! Yesterday I **(12)** .... the university tennis club with Jenny.

OK, that's enough for now. Write soon!

Jon

Vocabulary

education ▶ CB page 53

1 **Complete the sentences with the words in the box. You may need to change the form of some words.**

course   curriculum   homework
lecture hall   lecturer   module   project
report   research   seminar   teacher

1 I love my .... at school – her classes are really interesting and she always gives us a big .... to do at the end of term.

2 I hate doing .... every night – I'd much rather spend time after school with my friends.

3 I feel really nervous talking in a ...., but my university .... is kind and helps a lot.

4 I'm enjoying taking my .... in politics at college – I have to do a lot of .... on my own but that's very interesting.

5 I'm a bit nervous about my end-of-year .... from my teachers – it may not be very good!

6 The school .... includes German, art and music classes.

7 The course is organised in short .... Students have to choose four for the first year.

8 The .... on computer engineering will be held on 15 October. If you would like to attend, contact Professor Wilkins.

2 **Find and correct the spelling mistakes in the sentences. There are two mistakes in some sentences.**

1 It's easyer to put more efort into doing things I enjoy than things I don't.

2 I find it hard to concantrate in class when it's hot.

3 I've been making good progres with my Maths recently.

4 I'm planning to rejister for evning classes next term.

5 My friend doesn't atend every class – she's going to get into truble soon.

6 It's cleer that you have to study hard to pass exams.

adverbs ▶ CB page 53

3 **Complete the sentences with adverbs formed from the words in brackets.**

1 I .... (origin) wanted to be a dancer but now I'd like to be a teacher instead.

2 I get so annoyed when other students in the class are .... (continual) asking questions!

3 My friend passed the exam .... (easy).

4 It's difficult to explain the problem but, ... (basic), it's because of a computer breakdown.

5 .... (broad) speaking, the project is going to involve the whole department.

6 The lecturer is great – she explains everything so .... (clear) that we all understand it.

7 He worked .... (hard) to pass the exam.

8 My friend works .... (considerable) harder than I do!

4 **The adverb is in the wrong place in the sentences below. Find and correct the mistakes.**

1 The students looked very confused and didn't understand obviously the teacher.

2 Students have to hard work to finish their course.

3 The new computer room is great but it's just unfortunately for older students.

4 My friend can well speak French.

5 The lesson clearly was too difficult for most of the students in the class.

6 There is one student in my class continually who is talking – the teacher gets very cross.

Listening
True/False (Part 4) ▶ CB page 54

1 **Match the first half of the sentences (1–5) with the second (A–E).**

1 It's important to have good dress sense

2 A good manager should have

3 Schools should teach money management

4 Living healthily involves many things

5 An important skill for a leader is

A being good at decision-making.

B like diet, exercise and rest.

C to look good when you have a job interview.

D good communication skills and be able to talk to staff.

E so children don't have financial problems later on.

2 **Choose the correct alternative in each sentence.**

1 The instructor often *gets / becomes* cross with me.

2 I *found / discovered* the theory of driving quite easy.

3 I *passed / succeeded* my theory test.

4 It's difficult to *deal with / manage* traffic on the road.

5 I *spent / used* a lot of time practising for my test.

6 I'm *taking / getting* my driving test next week.

3 ▶ **23 You will hear two friends, George and Janet, talking about learning to drive. What topics do you think they might discuss? Tick (✓) three, then listen and check your answers.**

1 parking   4 cyclists

2 maintenance   5 speed cameras

3 theory test

4 **Listen again and decide if each sentence is correct or incorrect. If it is correct, put a tick (✓) in the box under A for YES. If it is incorrect, put a tick (✓) in the box under B for NO.**

		A	B
1	George is happy with his driving instructor.	☐	☐
2	Janet feels confident about driving past people on bicycles.	☐	☐
3	George found it easy to pass the theory test.	☐	☐
4	Janet is most nervous about parking.	☐	☐
5	George sometimes feels embarrassed when he is driving.	☐	☐
6	Janet is considering delaying her driving test.	☐	☐

Speaking

Personal questions (Part 1) ▶ CB page 55

1 ▶ 24 **Listen to part of a conversation between two candidates and an examiner. Tick (✓) the topics the examiner asks the candidates about.**

1 where they live   4 what they like doing in their spare time
2 their families   5 their plans for the future
3 their studies

2 **Here are some comments examiners wrote about candidates. Which comment is about the two candidates you listened to?**

A *Both candidates answered my questions but they also explained what their answers meant by giving more specific information.*

B Neither of these candidates seemed to really understand my questions. They didn't ask me to repeat what I had said either.

C These candidates only answered my questions even when I tried to get them to give me more specific information. It was as if they didn't want me to hear their English.

3 **Listen again and complete the sentences from the conversation with the words in the box.**

| anyway | as a matter of fact | I mean | like |
| mind you | well | well, you know | you know |

1 ...., I've just finished studying at an art school.
2 ...., I want to study something else, like a Master's degree.
3 ...., I work and I study.
4 I work, ..., part-time in a café.
5 ...., it can be a bit difficult at times.
6 ...., the normal things that young people like to do.
7 ...., we enjoy just being together.
8 I mean, ... going to clubs or maybe going round to a friend's house for a meal.

Grammar

past perfect simple ▶ CB page 56

1 **Choose the correct alternatives to complete the text.**

As soon as I **(1)** *got* / *had got* to university, I remembered that my classmates **(2)** *told* / *had told* me there was going to be an exam that day. I **(3)** *felt* / *had felt* really nervous because I **(4)** *missed* / *had missed* lots of lectures and I really **(5)** *didn't know* / *hadn't known* much about the subject at all.

By the time I **(6)** *got* / *had got* to the lecture hall, the lecturer **(7)** *already gave out* / *had already given out* the exam papers. I **(8)** *didn't have* / *hadn't had* anything for breakfast and I **(9)** *didn't feel* / *hadn't felt* very well. Most of the other students **(10)** *seemed* / *had seemed* to be finding the exam quite easy. I **(11)** *barely looked* / *had barely looked* at the questions when I **(12)** *saw* / *had seen* that the boy next to me **(13)** *wrote* / *had written* almost a page.

When the lecturer **(14)** *said* / *had said* to stop writing, I **(15)** *only answered* / *had only answered* two of the three questions. I **(16)** *was* / *had been* sure I **(17)** *failed* / *had failed* but when the results **(18)** *came out* / *had come out*, I **(19)** *saw* / *had seen* that I **(20)** *got* / *had got* quite a good mark!

2 **Join the sentences. Begin with the words in brackets and change the verbs to the correct form.**

1 I woke up. I missed my doctor's appointment. (*by the time*)
2 Adam collected his luggage. He went to look for a taxi. (*as soon as*)
3 Heather finished doing her homework. She went out. (*when*)
4 We did the shopping. We came home and cleaned the house. (*after*)
5 Christine got to the beach. It started to rain. (*by the time*)
6 He blew out the candles on the birthday cake. He started opening his presents. (*as soon as*)
7 Stephen finished his breakfast. His sister left for school. (*by the time*)
8 The teacher arrived. The students already stopped talking. (*when*)

Writing

Story (Part 3) ▶ CB page 57

1 **Look at the exam task and the story a candidate has written. Find and correct six mistakes with the past simple and the past perfect.**

Your English teacher has asked you to write a story. Your story must begin with this sentence:

It was my first day.

Write your story in about 100 words.

It was my first day. My mother hung my new school uniform in the wardrobe the night before. She put my new school shoes next to the chest of drawers. The next morning, after I had my shower, I started to get dressed. Suddenly, I realised that my school shoes hadn't been there. It was only then that I had remembered that I had left my bedroom door open the night before. I ran downstairs and out into the back garden. There was our new puppy, Eddie, with one of my new school shoes in his mouth! He already destroyed the other shoe.

2 **Divide the story in Activity 1 into paragraphs.**

3 **Complete sentences 1–9 to make a story. Use one idea from each of the boxes on the right.**

1 It was my first day …
2 I was feeling …
3 In fact, something rather strange had happened …
4 I had been …
5 I decided …
6 I was still thinking about what had happened when I …
7 I tried …
8 Finally, I …
9 We …

4 **Write a final sentence for your story.**

1
- at university.
- in a completely new job.
- on holiday with my friends.

2
- nervous because I'd never had a proper job before.
- a little bit anxious but also curious about the other students, the lecturers and the course.
- really great because I knew we were going to have a really fantastic time.

3
- a few days before.
- the night before.
- exactly a year before.

4
- looking at clothes in a shop I really like when I saw a boy I know trying to steal a leather jacket.
- in bed for about an hour when I heard someone outside the house calling out my name.
- on my way to the airport when I realised I had left my passport at home.

5
- to ignore it and soon after I fell asleep.
- to call out his name and he was so embarrassed that he put the jacket back.
- not to go and get it because I knew I could travel on my national ID.

6
- realised that the lecturer was asking me a question.
- realised that I had left my small backpack at home with all my favourite clothes in it.
- saw the boss standing in front of my desk.

7
- to phone my mother but I didn't have enough credit on my phone to make an international call.
- to pretend I had been thinking about the latest sales figures but I don't think he believed me.
- to remember the last thing I had heard her say but my mind was a complete blank.

8
- decided to admit that I hadn't been listening.
- managed to send her a text message and she promised to post it to me the next day.
- asked him a question about the company and he seemed to be pleased about that.

9
- went on talking about company policy for the next 20 minutes or so.
- finished the lecture and she smiled at me as she went out of the room.
- went to the post office every day for a week but the backpack never arrived.

Water

Listening

Multiple choice (Part 2) ▶ CB page 60

1 Match verbs 1–6 with phrases A–F to make collocations.

1	run	A	the flowers in the garden
2	pour	B	your clothes
3	have	C	a bath
4	rinse	D	a cup of tea
5	water	E	your hair after using shampoo
6	wash	F	a shower

2 ▶ 25 **You will hear part of an interview with a woman called Nadia Winters, who presents the weather forecast on television. For each question, mark the correct letter, A, B, or C.**

1 How did Nadia feel about science at school?
  A She enjoyed all aspects of it.
  B She preferred to study other subjects.
  C She needed to do it for her future work plans.

2 What does Nadia say about being on television?
  A Her parents encouraged her to try it.
  B She had always wanted to do it.
  C She was nervous about it.

3 Nadia says that she got her first job presenting the weather on television because
  A she worked hard.
  B another presenter left.
  C she knew the right people.

4 What does Nadia like best about her job?
  A being famous
  B meeting different people
  C travelling around the country

5 What does Nadia say about being a TV weather presenter?
  A It's important to be confident.
  B It's easier if you are an actor as well.
  C It's necessary to understand the technical details.

6 Nadia says that it's hard to give detailed weather forecasts
  A in the long winter months.
  B during very windy weather.
  C when it is a long way in the future.

Grammar

countable and uncountable nouns
▶ CB page 61

1 Write the words in the box in the correct column to complete the table.

---
advice   book   coffee   frost   glass   kilometre
language   lesson   noise   rain   raindrop
smoke   snow   snowflake   steam
---

countable	uncountable	both

2 Choose the correct alternative in each sentence.

1 *Many / Much* people enjoy going on cruises because they are very relaxing.

2 Cruise ships have *a lot of / much* activities on board.

3 People on cruise ships sometimes think there is too *many / much* to do!

4 *Few / Little* people dislike going on cruises.

5 Some people spend *a lot of / many* time on cruises.

6 The ship's engines didn't make *much / few* noise.

3 Put the words in the box into the correct sentence. You may need to change the form of some words. There is one word you do not need to use.

---
bread   coffee   glass (x2)   noise (x2)   painting
---

1 At night you can hear some very strange .... on a ship!

2 It's important to keep the .... in the portholes clean so that passengers can see out.

3 I can't see anything if I don't wear my ....

4 I often buy .... at the supermarket even though it's not as good as the baker's.

5 I sometimes buy .... I like in art galleries – and they often sell art on cruise ships.

6 I really hate it when there's a lot of .... at night – I can't sleep!

Vocabulary

weather   ▶ CB page 62

1 Do the crossword.

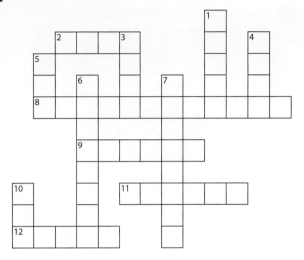

Across

2 white frozen water that falls from the sky

8 a storm with thunder and lightning

9 a short period of rain or snow

11 a word that means 'just a little bit cold'

12 very strong winds

Down

1 thin ice that forms in very low temperatures

3 air that moves and blows about

4 a verb to describe how heavy rain falls

5 another word for 'rainy'

6 bright light from the sun, good for sunbathing

7 a word that means 'extremely cold'

10 cloudy air near the ground which is difficult to see through

2 Complete the sentences with words from the crossword in Activity 1 in the correct form.

1 There'll be some .... tonight so drive slowly – you won't be able to see very far ahead.

2 There is often a .... at the end of a hot summer day, with bright lightning.

3 In the winter, when it's very cold, there is often a .... in the early morning.

4 When I'm on holiday, I want lots of .... so that I can get a tan!

5 I hate very strong .... – they can often cause damage to houses.

6 We can't go out yet – it's .... with rain.

Speaking

Simulated situation (Part 2)
▶ CB page 63

1 Look at the exam task and decide if these sentences are true or false.

1 You have to choose the best type of film.
2 You have to decide which setting would be best.

> I'm going to describe a situation to you. A famous director is planning to make a disaster movie. He is trying to decide which one of these settings would be best. Talk together about the settings and decide which would be the most suitable for a disaster movie.

2 ▶ 26 Read the comments an examiner wrote about two candidates. Then listen to the candidates, Martin and Ana, talking about the settings in Activity 1 and match them with the comments. Write *M* (*Martin*) or *A* (*Ana*) next to each comment.

1 used some good vocabulary to describe the first two settings
2 in too much of a hurry to reach a conclusion
3 didn't really try to get the other candidate to talk
4 seems to have good language skills but I didn't hear enough to be sure

3 Here are some extracts from a conversation about the same task between two other candidates. Complete them with the words in the box. There is one word you do not need to use.

agree   and   how about   right   think
what   why

1 I think the cruise ship would be a good setting. Do you ....?

2 So you think it would be too much like *Titanic*. ....'s that?

3 Do you .... the rainstorm or the killer shark would be more exciting?

4 I see what you mean about the wave. .... the surfers? What would happen to them?

5 Maybe it could be a modern version of *Titanic* on a megaship. .... do you think?

6 So we both think the giant surf would make the most exciting setting. Is that ....?

4 Now match extracts 1–6 from Activity 3 with responses A–F below.

A Perhaps, but there have already been lots of movies in settings like that. *Titanic*, for example.

B Great! Filming on a megaship would make it more original and up-to-date.

C Yes. Let's go for the surf setting.

D Well, they could try and surf the wave and manage to get to shore. That would be really exciting.

E I prefer the rainstorm myself. Weren't there a whole lot of movies about a killer shark ages ago?

F Well, it's a film about a ship. And the most famous film about a ship is *Titanic*, isn't it?

Reading

True/False (Part 3) ▶ CB page 64

1 You are going to read an article about how to survive on a deserted island. Read the article quickly and put these items in the order in which they appear in the text. Number them 1 to 8.

A the wind
B cuts
C waterfalls and streams
D saltwater
E insects
F a message
G passing ships or boats
H leaves

2 Look at the sentences about surviving on a deserted island. Read the article again to decide if each sentence is correct or incorrect. If it is correct, mark it A. If it is incorrect, mark it B.

A B

1 Finding food is just as important as finding water. ☐ ☐
2 Water you find in places other than waterfalls or streams can make you sick. ☐ ☐
3 Green coconut juice can be poisonous. ☐ ☐
4 Drinking sea water stops your liver working. ☐ ☐
5 Your shelter shouldn't block your view of the sea. ☐ ☐
6 You only need to build a fire if you plan to cook. ☐ ☐
7 You shouldn't eat the insects on the island even if you are desperate. ☐ ☐
8 Coconuts are a good source of protein. ☐ ☐
9 If you put coconut oil on a cut, it can get infected. ☐ ☐
10 You should put a message in a bottle and hope that someone will find it. ☐ ☐

3 Look at the words in bold in the article and choose the correct definition for each word.

1 tips: *money you give to a waiter / useful pieces of advice*
2 grab: *take quickly / hold tightly*
3 shelter: *hiding place / protection*
4 chilly: *cold / frightening*
5 choosy: *careful / fussy*
6 soothe: *make it feel better / protect*

SURVIVING ON A DESERTED ISLAND

Would you know what to do if you found yourself alone on a deserted tropical island? It can happen so it's worth being prepared. Here are some **tips**.

Your first priority is to look for drinking water. People can live without food for several weeks but will die in only a couple of days if they don't get enough liquid. Go inland from the beach and look for high rocks where there may be waterfalls or streams. The water in these will be purer and less likely to make you sick. Since this is a tropical island, there are probably loads of coconut palms around. Climb a tree and **grab** a couple of green coconuts. The liquid inside them is like a natural sports drink. It's full of potassium and other minerals, and it is a very good way of fighting dehydration. You should also try to find a way to collect any rainwater. You can use coconut shells or large leaves from tropical plants. Whatever you do, don't drink saltwater. The salt will make you even thirstier than you were before. In the end, it will cause kidney failure and kill you.

Next you should try to create some shelter. It is best if this is close to the beach so you can still see any passing ships or boats that might come to your rescue. Your **shelter** should protect you from the sun, wind and rain. You can use the branches of trees and palm leaves, which also make a soft place to sleep and can be used as blankets. It can be **chilly** at night so start preparing to make a fire. Apart from keeping you warm, you will need the fire to cook and it is also an excellent way of attracting attention.

By this stage you will be getting hungry. You can try fishing or hunting but insects are also a very good source of protein. You might not feel like eating these on your first day but, eventually, you won't be so **choosy**. Coconuts are another food you should make the most of. Apart from its high protein content, coconut flesh is full of vitamins and minerals and the oil can be used to **soothe** sunburnt skin and treat cuts.

Your main task now is to attract attention. Instead of putting a message in a bottle, use large stones to write one on the sand. It should be visible from the air. Keep your fingers crossed that someone will see it and come to your rescue!

Vocabulary

adjectives + prepositions ▶ CB page 64

1 **Match the first half of the sentences (1–10) with the second (A–J).**

1 Cats are not very keen
2 I'm not very familiar
3 Chicago is famous
4 Will people ever get tired
5 Tim's band is very similar
6 Tina got involved
7 I'm sometimes amazed
8 A lot of people are not very interested
9 I know my grandmother is very fond
10 Are the students getting worried

A with this part of the city.
B in a research project about saving water.
C of using the internet?
D by how much English I have actually learnt.
E on water.
F in politics nowadays.
G to some of the bands from the sixties.
H about their exams?
I for its skyscrapers and lake.
J of me and my cousins.

2 **Find and correct the mistakes with prepositions in the sentences. There are mistakes in seven of the sentences. Tick (✓) the sentences that are correct.**

1 Thailand and Greece are famous for their many beautiful islands.
2 I was amazed for how warm the water was in Thailand.
3 I'm very keen about swimming.
4 I don't think I'll ever get tired with going to the beach.
5 One of the beaches on Fuerteventura is similar to a beach I used to go to when I was a child.
6 Would you be interested for visiting Fuerteventura?
7 I know the north of the island quite well but I'm not as familiar on the south.
8 My friend who lives there is very involved about a campaign to keep the beaches clean.
9 She's very worried about threats to the environment.
10 We're both very fond with animals too.

Grammar

articles ▶ CB page 66

1 **Choose the correct alternative in each sentence.**

1 Do you ask your friends for *advice / the advice*?
2 There was *a thunderstorm / the thunderstorm* last night and *a noise / the noise* woke me up.
3 *Glass / The glass* is made from sand and other minerals.
4 Where there's *smoke / a smoke*, there's *fire / the fire*.
5 Could you get *bread / a bread* and some butter when you go out?
6 *Coffee / The coffee* they make here is always very strong.
7 Save *water / the water* and turn off *tap / the tap*.
8 I love *cheese / a cheese* but I don't like *milk / the milk*.

2 **Complete the text with *a, an, the* or – (= no article).**

Nobody knows exactly when **(1)** _____ people first started to build **(2)** _____ boats but it seems that **(3)** _____ history of sailing goes back thousands of years. **(4)** _____ very first boats were probably log canoes. **(5)** _____ boats capable of making **(6)** _____ long sea voyages are more recent but **(7)** _____ surprising discovery in **(8)** _____ unlikely place has provided more information. **(9)** _____ world's oldest sea-going boat was found in **(10)** _____ middle of **(11)** _____ desert in **(12)** _____ Kuwait. **(13)** _____ archaeologists who found it think it was used to carry goods from **(14)** _____ Mesopotamia to **(15)** _____ southern shores of **(16)** _____ Persian Gulf. This would explain why some Mesopotamian pottery was found thousands of miles from where it was made.

3 **Look at this postcard a candidate has written. The candidate has not used any articles. Put an article where necessary before the words in bold.**

Dear Marina,

We had **wonderful time** in **Egypt**. As you know, we took **cruise** down **Nile**. We started in **Cairo**. **Boat** was really luxurious and **itinerary** was amazing. We saw all **most famous** archaeological sites like **Pyramids of Giza** and **Valley of the Kings**. **Guides** were great and **other people** on **boat** were good fun. I tried to learn **bit of Arabic** but everyone spoke good English. On **last night** there was **special party** with **fantastic food** and **wonderful music**. By **time** we got to **bed**, **sun** had already come up!

Love,
Carla

Writing
Informal letter (Part 3) ▶ CB page 67

1 Look at the exam task, the letter a candidate has written and the examiner's comments. Match the examiner's comments (1–9) with the underlined mistakes in the letter (A–I).

> This is part of a letter you have received from a friend, Sara.
>
> *You said you were going on another cruise this year. I suppose you're back now. Where did you go? What did you enjoy most? What did you do on board the cruise ship?*
>
> Now write a letter to Sarah, answering her questions.
>
> Write your letter in about 100 words.

Dear Sara,

You were right. We got back from the <u>cruze</u> Ⓐ last week. It was great. <u>We sailed from Barcelona</u> Ⓑ to <u>Balearic Islands</u> Ⓒ of Menorca, Mallorca, Ibiza and Formentera. Formentera was the best part for me. There is <u>fantastic hippy market</u> Ⓓ there and <u>I buy</u> Ⓔ some really cool earrings and some sandals. There <u>was</u> Ⓕ really nice people on board the ship and lots of games and competitions. I'm not very keen on that kind of thing though. I prefer to just lie on deck and look at <u>sea</u> Ⓖ. <u>Well, that's all my news.</u> Ⓗ Write soon and <u>say</u> Ⓘ me when you are coming to visit us.

Love,

Analise

① You should start a new paragraph here.
② Spelling.
③ Something missing here.
④ Wrong tense.
⑤ Something missing here too.
⑥ Wrong form.
⑦ Wrong word.
⑧ Something missing here too.
⑨ You should start a new paragraph here.

2 Rewrite the letter in Activity 1, correcting the underlined mistakes.

3 Now write your own answer to the exam task in Activity 1. Use the information about a cruise of Turkey and the Greek islands in the brochure below.

ROUTE

DAY 1: Athens to Istanbul.

DAY 2: City visit, Istanbul. See the Grand Bazaar and the Blue Mosque.

DAY 3: Sail to Mykonos.

DAY 4: Sail to Heraklion on Crete. Visit the famous ruins of Knossos.

Celebrity

8

Vocabulary

entertainment ▶ CB page 69

1 **Look at the photo below. Which words from the box would you NOT use to describe it?**

celebrity	wave	photographers	cameras	push	happy
rush	dress	glamorous	shoes	bag	sunglasses

2 **Match 1–9 with A–I to make compound nouns.**

1 rock   A opera
2 ballet   B clothes
3 stage   C star
4 soap   D show
5 stadium   E dancer
6 magazine   F actor
7 chat   G cover
8 designer   H concert
9 television   I commercials

3 **Complete the conversation with compound nouns from Activity 2 in the correct form. The first letter of each word is given.**

Mike: Did you see that TV programme last night – the **(1)** c.................... s.................... where the presenter talked to that **(2)** b.................... d....................? She's an interesting person.

Sara: Yes – she left classical dancing to become a **(3)** r.................... s...................., didn't she? Imagine going from a classical stage with other dancers to giving a **(4)** s.................... c.................... in front of thousands of rock music fans!

Mike: But ballet is so different from rock music. I could have understood it if she had become a **(5)** s.................... a.................... in a theatre – after all, ballet involves acting, so that would be logical, and she's used to being on stage.

Sara: Yes. And sometimes dancers have chosen to appear in television **(6)** s.................... o.................... – just one episode, for the fun of acting in a popular series.

Mike: And, of course, other celebrities make **(7)** t.................... c.................... – they make a lot of money that way.

Sara: Then their photograph appears on **(8)** m.................... c.................... all over the world – it must be a great life. They get to wear expensive **(9)** d.................... c.................... and stay in five star hotels!

Mike: I'd love that! Some people seem to have all the luck.

Speaking

Extended turn (Part 3)   ▶ CB page 69

1 Look at the instructions and photos an examiner gave two candidates and what one of the candidates said. Which of the two photos is the candidate describing?

> I'm going to give you each a photograph of people taking photographs of celebrities. Candidate A, please tell us what you can see in the photograph.

(1) .... the middle of the photo there is a celebrity and she is wearing a beautiful dress. (2) .... the background there are other celebrities, men and women, who are wearing nice clothes too – everyone looks very smart. (3) .... the left-hand side of the photo there are a lot of cameras – the photographers are taking pictures of the celebrity, who is standing (4) .... front of the cameras looking at them. She looks happy. (5) .... the right-hand side of the photo I can see a statue – so it is a special event like the Oscars. (6) .... the top of the photo there is a glass roof.

2 Complete the candidate's description in Activity 1 with *in*, *on* or *at*.

3 Write a short description of the second photo in Activity 2. Use the phrases in the box and *there's …, there are …, I can see …* and *we can see … .*

---
at the top of the photo   in front of the camera
in the background   in the middle of the photo
on the left-/right-hand side of the photo
---

4 ▶ 27 Listen to a candidate describing the second photo in Activity 2. Check that you mentioned the same things in your description.

General conversation (Part 4)
▶ CB page 69

5 Look at the instructions an examiner gave two candidates and what the candidates said. Did they follow the examiner's instructions?

> Your photographs both showed famous celebrities. Now I'd like you to talk together about which celebrities you admire and why you admire them.

A: I love Michael Cera. I think *Arrested Development* is great.

B: Sorry? What did you say the name of the show was?

A: *Arrested Development*.

B: I don't think it's on in my country. What's he like?

A: Oh he's brilliant! Do you have a favourite actor?

B: Well, there are lots of people I like. Hailee Steinfeld, for example. She's won loads of awards for her acting. What about musicians?

A: I used to be really into Cody Simpson but I'm not so keen on him now. What do you think of Selena Gómez?

B: I bet you like her! I can't stand Justin Bieber but don't mind her, actually. Did you know that she's like a UNICEF ambassador or something?

A: No, I didn't. I think it's great that she does charity work but I just love her music and I think she's really pretty. Is there anyone else you like?

B: Loads of people. You can't beat a good boy band!

6 Now look at the advice the teacher gave the candidates before the exam. Did the candidates follow the advice?

1 Make sure you ask the other candidate questions to try and get them to talk.

2 Show interest in what the other candidate says.

3 Don't talk to the examiner – talk to each other.

4 If you don't understand what the other candidate says, ask them to repeat it.

7 Find expressions in the conversation in Activity 5 to match these meanings.

1 I don't like X so much.

2 I'm sure you like X.

3 I used to like X.

4 There is nothing better than X.

5 I don't like or dislike X.

6 I really dislike X.

Reading

Multiple-choice cloze (Part 5)
▶ CB page 70

1 **Read the article quickly and choose the best title for it.**

A Why people are interested in celebrities

B The secret life of celebrities

C A celebrity lifestyle

| 50 |

Everyone needs someone to **(0)** _A look_ up to – a role model. While it would be ideal if we were all fascinated by **(1)** .... who have achieved something worthwhile, sadly, the **(2)** .... of us aren't. Media outlets like TV, mobile phones and the internet spread information about reality TV stars but not charity workers. And **(3)** .... such stars should have talent, they often don't. There are many who can **(4)** .... act nor sing but are still celebrities. This is depressing!

So **(5)** .... do we find them interesting? It's because we dream of becoming rich and famous ourselves. We try to escape from everyday life because we don't want to **(6)** .... our time doing a boring job. We follow the glamorous lives of celebrities on social networking sites and in newspaper **(7)** .... because we want to be them. But this trend is worrying. In **(8)** .... , it's reached a point where celebrities have turned **(9)** .... products or brands that can be sold. The real question is **(10)** .... being a celebrity is really an amazing achievement at all!

---

2 **Read the article in Activity 1 again and choose the correct word for each space. For each question, mark the correct letter A, B, C or D.**

3 **Underline three compound nouns in the article in Activity 1.**

4 **Find words in the article in Activity 1 to match definitions 1–8.**

1 perfect

2 useful and valuable

3 natural ability

4 sad; making you miserable

5 avoid something bad or unpleasant

6 rich and exciting

7 fashion, movement

8 something important that you do successfully

Vocabulary

-ed and -ing adjectives ▶ CB page 71

1 **Choose the correct alternatives to complete the rules.**

1 When an adjective describes a person's feelings, it ends in -ed / -ing.

2 When an adjective describes a thing that affects a person's feelings, it ends in -ed / -ing.

2 **Complete the sentences with adjectives formed from the verbs in brackets.**

1 It's rather .... (depress) when things keep going wrong.

2 I am .... (fascinate) by the lives of celebrities – I can't stop reading about them!

3 I find it .... (surprise) that so many people read about celebrities.

4 I get very .... (bore) by reading about talentless people.

5 There's a very .... (interest) programme on television tonight about celebrities.

6 It's very .... (encourage) when people tell you you're doing things well.

7 I'm .... (amaze) you've never heard of her – she's really famous!

8 It's .... (worry) that such talentless people are role models for so many young people nowadays.

0	**A** look	**B** see	**C** watch	**D** view
1	**A** they	**B** them	**C** those	**D** their
2	**A** much	**B** most	**C** many	**D** majority
3	**A** although	**B** however	**C** since	**D** despite
4	**A** either	**B** neither	**C** none	**D** nothing
5	**A** why	**B** when	**C** where	**D** how
6	**A** bring	**B** take	**C** give	**D** spend
7	**A** adverts	**B** articles	**C** chapters	**D** essays
8	**A** front	**B** case	**C** fact	**D** order
9	**A** into	**B** out	**C** up	**D** by
10	**A** unless	**B** does	**C** what	**D** whether

3 Complete the sentences with adjectives formed from the verbs in the box.

bore	depress	encourage	fascinate
frighten	interest	surprise	worry

1 I feel rather .... when the newspapers are full of pointless articles about celebrities.

2 The lives of rich people are .... – they are so different from mine!

3 I get very .... when celebrities do a lot of charity work.

4 I'm not at all .... in what rich people do.

5 Most celebrities are pretty .... people, in my opinion. I'm not interested in them.

6 It's .... how many young people are only interested in becoming famous.

7 I was pleasantly .... when I read about the charity work celebrities often do.

8 Are you at all .... by the intense media interest in celebrities?

4 Find and correct the mistakes in the sentences. There are mistakes in four of the sentences. Tick (✓) the sentences that are correct.

1 I love reading about famous people – it's fascinated!

2 I find the media quite depressed – it's always bad news or celebrities!

3 It's encouraging when people praise things you do.

4 I get very bored by some things – like reading about talentless people.

5 Are you interesting in films?

6 Do you get worried when things go wrong?

7 I often get frightening by horror films!

8 My friend loves reading about celebrities – she's fascinated by them.

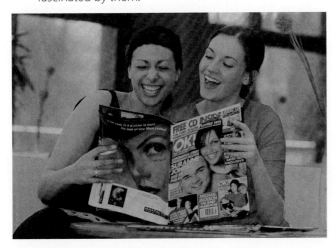

Grammar
reported speech ▶ CB page 72

1 Rewrite the sentences in reported speech.

1 'I saw Mylie Cyrus in an airport once.'
He said ....

2 'I met Emma Watson in a café in March!'
He said ....

3 'I don't believe him though.'
She said ....

4 'He's never met anyone famous.'
She said ....

5 'He's always saying that he's seen someone famous somewhere or other.'
She told me ....

6 'I've been to the Academy Awards ceremony a couple of times.'
She said ....

7 'It was amazing!'
She said ....

8 'I can't go this year because there's something really important I have to do that day.'
She told me ....

9 'I'll tell you if I'm going next year.'
She said ....

10 'You can join me!'
She said ....

2 Find and correct the mistakes in the sentences. Tick (✓) the sentences that are correct.

1 He told us that he could speak Japanese.

2 She said me she didn't like having her photo taken.

3 She told she would be at home on Saturday night.

4 My singing coach said I had to practise more.

5 I told them that I didn't want to be on a TV show.

6 Carla said us she had tried to get a part in a movie.

7 Liam said I could borrow his camera.

8 Luke said me he would be late for the interview.

9 She told to me that she was going home.

10 Tim said he had been late for school the day before.

3 What were the people's actual words in Activity 2? Rewrite the sentences in direct speech.

4 Read part of an interview with Sean, an Australian actor, and the article Kim, the journalist, wrote based on the interview. Then complete Kim's article below.

Kim: So, Sean, you grew up in Melbourne, Australia.

Sean: Not exactly. My family moved out of the city to a place called Apollo Bay. It was a great place to grow up!

Kim: And why was that?

Sean: My dad and all my brothers have always surfed but down there we surfed before school every day and after school as well. Also, it's a small community and I've always loved small communities where you sort of know everyone.

Kim: So how did you get into acting?

Sean: My brother Raori got into it first. As a kid, I'd always loved movies but it wasn't like I dreamt of being an actor or anything. It wasn't until I was about 17 and I watched my brothers doing TV shows in Australia that I wanted to act myself. I started doing classes outside of school and then got a part in the series *Home Town*. I think you know the rest of the story.

Kim: And what do your surfing friends think about your acting career?

Sean: They've never really shown much interest in it, actually. They just want to go and surf so they don't treat me any differently.

Sean's still surfing!

I'm really impressed by Sean O'Sullivan! He hasn't forgotten where he comes from, even though he's now world famous. Sean told me that he **(1)** .... in a small town near Melbourne called Apollo Bay. Apparently, his family moved there to get away from the city. Sean loved living there. He said that his father and his brothers **(2)** .... and that in Apollo Bay they **(3)** .... after school every day!

Another thing he loves is the sense of community. He told me that because it was such a small place, he **(4)** .... almost everyone there.

I wasn't surprised to hear that Sean **(5)** .... movies as a child. But it did surprise me to learn that acting hadn't been one of his dreams. He told me that he **(6)** .... doing acting classes after school, when his brothers began appearing on TV shows in Australia.

He's stayed friends with his surfing mates over the years. Sean said they **(7)** .... much interest in his acting career and that all they **(8)** .... to do was surf. For the Apollo Bay surfers, Sean's still just one of the guys.

Listening

Gap-fill (Part 3)   ▶ CB page 73

1 Read the advert for a new television show and decide if the sentences are true or false.

New reality show coming to **Channel 10** later in the year! Watch **ordinary people** interview **celebrities** when they are **off-guard** and ask them **difficult questions**. See how they react! *The fun starts in August – make sure you're tuned in!*

1 The celebrities are expecting an interview.
2 The presenters are professional actors.
3 The programme begins in the summer.

2 ▶ 28 You will hear Paul Johnson, the producer of a new reality TV show, talking about ways of getting on the show. Listen and complete each gap in the leaflet with one word from the recording.

New reality TV show!

We're looking for new presenters to interview celebrities.

People required:
- Must be outgoing and good at communication.
- The best age for presenters is **(1)** ....

Qualifications and experience:
New presenters:
- get training on how to **(2)** .... and speak in a natural way.
- are given **(3)** .... to wear.
- must speak **(4)** .... as well as other languages.

How to apply:
Send an email with a **(5)** .... and your phone number.

Dates for auditions:
From 23 April to **(6)** .... April.

Grammar

reported questions ▶ CB page 74

1 **Rewrite the questions in reported speech. Begin with** *He asked me ... .*

1 'Do you find Brad Pitt attractive?'

2 'What do you like most about him?'

3 'Do you think he is more attractive than Johnny Depp?'

4 'What did you think of his latest film?'

5 'Was Angelina Jolie in it too?'

6 'Who else was in it?'

7 'Have you seen any of her films?'

8 'Are you going to the cinema this weekend?'

9 'Can I come with you?'

10 'How much will the tickets cost?'

2 **A candidate wrote these sentences about an interview he had. Find and correct the mistakes with reported questions in them. There are mistakes in six of the sentences. Tick (✓) the sentences that are correct.**

1 She asked me where did I live.

2 She asked me have you always lived there.

3 She wanted to know what it was like living there.

4 She also asked me what I am studying at the moment.

5 She asked me what I had done during the summer holidays.

6 She wanted to know if I had enjoyed myself.

7 She asked if I have got any special plans for the future.

8 She wanted to know what was I going to do when I finished studying.

9 She also asked me what I enjoyed doing with my friends in the evenings.

10 She wanted to know do I enjoy watching television or listening to music.

Writing

Story (Part 3) ▶ CB page 75

1 **Look at the exam task and the stories two candidates have written. Which of these tips for making your writing more interesting does each story follow?**

1 Set the scene.

2 Include the main events.

3 Write a good ending.

4 Divide your story into paragraphs.

5 Add some dialogue to make your story more exciting.

> Your English teacher has asked you to write a story.
> Your story must begin with this sentence:
> *I had always wanted to be famous until that day in March.*
> Write your story in about 100 words.

A I had always wanted to be famous until that day in March. A few weeks earlier I had been chosen to do a screen test for a new TV series. It turned out that I had to go to the TV studio for the test. I'd just arrived when a girl handed me a piece of paper. 'You've got ten minutes,' she said. 'Then you're on.' 'What do I have to do?' I asked. 'Read it!' she said, and rushed off. I suddenly remembered that I'd left my glasses at home. I heard the director call, 'Next!' but I couldn't do it.

B I had always wanted to be famous until that day in March. I noticed a photographer on a motorbike following a young woman wearing sunglasses. The photographer kept following her and taking photos. As I got closer, I realised it was the actress, Katharine McPhee.

A few days later I saw the photos on the internet. There were nasty comments about her clothes and her hair. It seemed really unfair. It must be terrible if you can't walk along the street without paparazzi following you. It made me feel sorry for celebrities and glad, for the first time in my life, that I am not famous!

2 **Write the stories again and improve them so that they both follow all the tips in Activity 1.**

Creativity

Speaking

Extended turn (Part 3) ▶ CB page 78

1 **Read the two conversations below and decide if these sentences about them are true or false.**

1 The man is thinking in an imaginative way.
2 The man is thinking in a logical way.
3 The woman is thinking in a creative way.
4 The woman is not thinking about different ideas.

> **Woman:** I've never made this meal before. Why don't we try putting in some sugar?
>
> **Man:** There isn't any sugar in the recipe so we shouldn't do it.
>
> **Woman:** But it might make it taste better. And it's fun to do something unexpected and try to change things!
>
> **Man:** Why are you getting on that bus? It's not the normal route.
>
> **Woman:** Because I always like to try different things, just to see what will happen!
>
> **Man:** But you might get lost.
>
> **Woman:** Or I might find a better route to work and save time.

2 ▶ **29 Listen to Peter, a college tutor, talking about thinking critically and thinking creatively. Decide if the sentences are true or false.**

Peter thinks that

1 teachers only concentrate on critical thinking.
2 people who think creatively can find more than one solution to a problem.
3 in the real world people only think creatively.
4 people who think creatively are able to solve problems more effectively.

3 **Which of the words in the box can be used to talk about creative thinking? Which can be used to talk about critical thinking?**

analyse	explore	logic	many solutions	one solution	search

4 **Match verbs 1–6 with nouns A–F to make collocations.**

1	make	**A**	a solution
2	analyse	**B**	a logical argument
3	build	**C**	a difference
4	search	**D**	an example
5	give	**E**	for an answer
6	come up with	**F**	a problem

5 Look at the exam task and the photos. Complete the descriptions from two candidates using one word in each gap.

> Look at the photographs of people and works of art. Candidate A, talk about what you can see in photograph A. Candidate B, listen, then talk about what you can see in photograph B.

Candidate A

In the middle of the photograph **(1)** ....'s a man sitting in **(2)** .... of a painting. I think he's an **(3)** .... He's **(4)** .... a T-shirt and a baseball cap, and he has a **(5)** .... I can't see **(6)** .... the painting is but it **(7)** .... like a lot of lines and strange shapes.

Candidate B

In the **(8)** .... of the photo there's a woman holding something – it looks **(9)** .... a fish. In the **(10)** .... there are some other strange things – maybe she made them herself. She **(11)** .... wearing jeans and a sweater, and she's smiling, **(12)** .... I think she's happy. On the right-hand **(13)** .... there's a plant but I don't know **(14)** .... it's called.

6 ▶ **30 Now listen to the candidates and check your answers to Activity 5.**

Grammar

modals of ability ▶ CB page 79

1 **Choose the correct alternative in each sentence.**

1 I *can / manage* to play the guitar but I *can't / couldn't* sing.

2 This painting is fantastic! *Can / Could* you paint in oils as well as draw?

3 I *could / managed* to get a ticket for tonight's concert at the last minute.

4 Brian *can't / couldn't* hear the phone ringing because he was watching a film on TV.

5 I *could / managed* to get quite a good photo of Jamie even though he never sits still.

6 *Will you be able to / Could you* join us tomorrow?

2 **There is one extra word in each of these sentences. Find it and cross it out.**

1 They were be able to see an island in the distance.

2 Did you could manage to finish that painting?

3 Could you to tell me where I can buy art materials?

4 Will you be able to manage come to the meeting?

5 My cousin is able to can design web pages.

6 We won't be not able to send you the tickets until next week.

3 **Complete the article. Use one word in each gap.**

The very young artist

If you ask most children to paint a street scene, they are usually only **(1)** .... to produce triangle-topped boxes for houses, stick trees and animals or people that are the wrong size. But one young boy is different. Although he is only six, Jamie **(2)** .... paint in a way that many adults **(3)** .... only feel jealous of. At first he painted boats and sea scenes and then realised he **(4)** .... also paint rural landscapes and animals. One art expert said it was unusual to find someone so young who **(5)** .... paint in this way.

Jamie says he likes painting because it's fun and because it helps him imagine places he **(6)** .... visit because they're too far away. He is hoping that he'll **(7)** .... able to have his own exhibition before he feels he is too old – that means at least before he is eight! It seems impossible but we're sure he **(8)** .... do it!

Reading
Matching (Part 2) ▶ CB page 80

1 The people below all want to take an art course. There are descriptions of eight courses. Decide which course (A–H) would be the most suitable for each person (1–5).

1   Carmen hasn't tried to paint or draw anything since she was a child. She doesn't have any of her own **materials**. She would like to take her time and go to the course once a week for a few months. ....

2   Adam wants to start making clothes for his friends. He would like to be able to show them pictures of what he plans to make first. He loves all the styles from the 1940s and often watches films from that time. ....

3   Paula learnt to paint at school and is very good at it. Recently she started a painting of her husband that she is having **trouble** finishing. She would prefer a course that only lasts a couple of days. ....

4   Daniel has been painting for many years. He would like to try something new. He loves music and often uses it to give him ideas. ....

5   Sam has always wanted to paint people. He can draw but he needs to learn how to use materials. He has his own **studio** at home. ....

Art courses

A Drawing from scratch
For absolute beginners, the course is a relaxed introduction to basic drawing skills. No experience needed, and paper and pencils supplied. Weekly sessions from January to June.

B Express yourself through drawing
Draw confidently and develop your ability to express yourself while learning about design. Draw from life or from your imagination.

C Fashion design
Learn to create attractive clothes. Find out how to draw an **outfit** and get inspiration from nature and from old movies. Great for students with a general interest in fashion design.

D Hat making
Learn to produce your own absolutely fabulous and original hat to match your favourite outfit! Course tutor Maggie Da Silva designed the hats for Channel 2's hit period drama *Upton Castle*.

E Oil painting
Learn to use oil paints like a professional artist. This course covers the main oil painting **techniques**. Your finished painting will be shown in the end-of-course exhibition.

F Painting portraits
By the end of this six-week course you will have made a good start on your first portrait, which you can then finish at home. You will learn about the relationship between colour and light, how to mix paints and how to use paintbrushes.

G Painting school
Over two consecutive days, experienced students develop their skills and find new artistic directions. Are you a bit **stuck** with something you've started to work on? Bring it along or start a new piece of work.

H Watercolour world
This course is suitable for experienced artists. Explore the possibilities that watercolour painting offers. Work from your own photographs or be inspired by nature or music.

2 **Match the words in bold in the texts on page 56 with definitions 1–6.**

1   a set of clothes that you wear together
2   unable to continue with your work because it is too difficult
3   a room where a painter or photographer works
4   special skills or ways of doing things
5   problems or difficulties
6   things you use in order to do an activity

Vocabulary

formal language   ▶ CB page 81

1 **Find less formal synonyms for these words in the texts on page 56.**

1   attempted (text 1)   4   required (text A)
2   intends (text 2)   5   exhibited (text E)
3   skilful (text 3)   6   complete (text F)

2 **Rewrite the sentences to make them less formal.**

1   Sonia is not a very good sculptor but she's an extremely skilful painter.
2   She has exhibited her work all over Europe and Asia.
3   She required a visa for some of the countries she visited.
4   I attempted to enrol in a course at the art college but my application arrived too late.
5   I hope to complete my studies early next year.
6   I intended to study painting and drawing.

3 **In the sentences below, both alternatives have a similar meaning. Choose the more formal alternative.**

1   If you *want* / *would like* to know more about the job, *tell us* / *let us know*.
2   The bus for London *sets off* / *departs* at 6 a.m.
3   For *further* / *more* information, please visit our website.
4   Any student who has *finished* / *completed* their task can leave now.
5   We *request* / *ask* that people close the windows when they leave the room.
6   We think that our course *provides students with* / *gives students* a good introduction to the workplace.

Listening

Multiple choice (Part 2)   ▶ CB page 82

1 **Match verbs 1–6 with nouns A–F to make collocations.**

1   work   A   realistic
2   get   B   your time
3   waste   C   a character
4   create   D   a job
5   have   E   in a team
6   look   F   a problem

2 ▶ **31 You will hear an interview with Brian, a computer games designer. For each question, mark the correct letter, A, B or C.**

1   Brian became a computer games designer because
    A   his family encouraged him.
    B   he got a job after graduation.
    C   he learnt a lot about it at college.

2   The thing Brian finds most difficult is
    A   getting original ideas.
    B   working with others.
    C   staying motivated.

3   What Brian enjoys most about designing games is
    A   making them look beautiful.
    B   producing them technically.
    C   seeing people playing them.

4   What does Brian think about *Village Games*?
    A   It was impossible to write the story.
    B   It was important to get the level right.
    C   It was the most popular game he designed.

5   What does Brian think about children playing computer games?
    A   They can develop useful skills.
    B   They should try other things like sport.
    C   They spend too much time playing computer games.

6   What does Brian say about good games designers?
    A   They have a lot of patience.
    B   They are good players themselves.
    C   They understand people's personalities.

Grammar

relative clauses ▶ CB page 83

1 Choose the correct alternatives to complete the article.

Drawing on the brain

In the late 1960s Betty Edwards, **(1)** *who / that* was an art teacher, began to wonder why her students, **(2)** *who / which* had successfully learnt languages, mathematics and other skills, found it so hard to learn to draw. She had also noticed that some students **(3)** *who / what* had found it really difficult at the beginning suddenly seemed to be able to draw perfectly well. She began to explore the brain research **(4)** *who / that* had been done by a famous scientist called Roger Sperry. Sperry was one of the people **(5)** *who / which* were responsible for discovering that the brain is divided into two halves, or hemispheres. Edwards developed a theory based on the research **(6)** *who / that* Sperry had done and in 1979 she wrote a book, **(7)** *that / which* she called *The New Drawing on the Right Side of the Brain*. The book, **(8)** *who / which* you can still buy today, has helped thousands of people learn to draw.

2 Join the sentences using non-defining relative clauses. Use the underlined sentence for the relative clause.

1 <u>Joseph Conrad is one of the world's greatest writers in English</u>. He was not a native speaker of that language.

2 His father died when Joseph was only 11. <u>He had translated Shakespeare's plays into Polish</u>.

3 Joseph then lived with his uncle. <u>His uncle was a very careful man</u>.

4 However, he let the boy go away to sea. <u>He was only 16 at the time</u>.

5 His experiences on board ships inspired many of his novels. <u>The ships sailed to countries like India, Africa and Australia</u>.

3 Read the sentences and add commas where necessary.

1 My friend Stephanie who I met in France is from the north of England.

2 To celebrate her birthday which is next week we are all going out for lunch.

3 Then we are all going to see an exhibition at a gallery where they always have fantastic exhibitions.

4 The artist whose paintings we are going to see is called David Hockney.

5 His paintings which are so big they cover whole walls are mainly of the north of England.

6 After the end of May when the exhibition finishes it will only be possible to see the paintings in New York.

Vocabulary

job skills ▶ CB page 84

1 Look at the photos and choose the best word to complete each sentence about them.

1 This *job / work* is a very important one. He has to be very *careful / caring*.

2 He has to work very *long / big* hours.

3 He has to wear a *uniform / suit*.

4 He has to do a lot of *training / practising* to do this.

5 She needs to know a lot about different *kinds / bits* of music and *records / disks*.

6 She loves *listening / listening to* music.

7 Her clothes must be very *fashionable / new*.

8 She probably *studied / examined* music at college.

2 ▶ 32 **Listen to three people talking about their jobs. What do they do? Match each speaker with a job from the box.**

dentist   DJ   fire-fighter   games designer
pilot   politician   scientist   secretary
surgeon   teacher

3 **Listen again. What skill does each person like using most in their job? Choose a skill from the box for each speaker. There is a skill you do not need to use.**

attention to detail   communication skills
leadership skills   problem solving   teamwork

prefixes   ▶ CB page 84

4 **Choose a meaning from the box for each prefix.**

again   not (x4)   personal

1   im-   ....
2   un-   ....
3   re-   ....
4   dis-   ....
5   irr-   ....
6   self- ....

5 **Write the opposites of the words using prefixes.**

1   happy   ....
2   agree   ....
3   well   ....
4   regular   ....
5   employment   ....
6   like   ....
7   interesting   ....
8   possible   ....
9   patient   ....
10 advantage   ....

6 **Complete the conversations with words formed with prefixes from Activity 4.**

1   **A:** Do people say that you are not very patient?
    B: Yes, they think I'm very ....!

2   **A:** Would you like to do my job?
    B: No, I'd really .... it!

3   **A:** Are you feeling well?
    B: No, I'm feeling rather ...., I'm afraid.

4   **A:** Would you like to work for yourself one day?
    B: Yes, I'd love to be ....!

5   **A:** Would you like to change your job, even if you had to train again and get new skills?
    B: Oh yes, I'd love to .... and get new skills!

6   **A:** I don't think it's possible to finish this project.
    B: I agree – it's ....

7   **A:** I never know when you're at work – your hours are not at all regular.
    B: No, I work very .... hours, I know.

8   **A:** You don't look very happy about the news.
    B: No, I feel very .... about it.

Writing

Sentence transformations (Part 1)
▶ CB page 85

1 **Here are some sentences about starting out as a DJ. Complete the second sentence so that it means the same as the first. Use no more than three words.**

1   People think it's very exciting to work as a DJ.
    People think .... as a DJ is very exciting.

2   People expect you to know a lot about music.
    You are .... know a lot about music.

3   Some clubs won't hire you if you don't have your own equipment.
    Some clubs won't hire you .... you have your own equipment.

4   You need to have two CD players, headphones and a mixer.
    It .... for you to have two CD players, headphones and a mixer.

5   Any other equipment is less important.
    Any other equipment is not .... important.

What's it worth?

Listening

Gap-fill (Part 3) ▶ CB page 86

1 ⏵ 33 Listen and write the words you hear. Then check the spelling of the words in a dictionary.

1 .... 3 .... 5 .... 7 .... 9 ....

2 .... 4 .... 6 .... 8 .... 10 ....

2 ⏵ 34 You will hear a man giving information on the radio about a sale taking place at a hotel. Listen and complete each gap in the leaflet with one word from the recording.

➤ Location: **(1)** .... Hotel
➤ Cheapest parking costs: **(2)** £........................
➤ **(3)** .... will be the most popular items for sale.
➤ The sale starts at **(4)** .... a.m. on Saturday.
➤ Older people should bring their **(5)** .... card.
➤ Detailed information can be found in the local **(6)** ....

Grammar

passive voice ▶ CB page 87

1 You are going to read about some things that were sold on the internet. Read the article on page 61 and choose the best answer to the questions.

1 Who might find the cookie jar useful?

  A cooks

  B people on a diet

  C science fiction enthusiasts

2 What is the biggest selling point of the USB typewriter?

  A It was invented a long time ago.

  B It combines features of the past and the present.

  C It is easy to use.

2 Read the article again and decide if the sentences are true or false, or if there is no information in the text.

1 The cookie jar was designed to stop people taking biscuits.

2 The cookie jar was made in China.

3 The cookie jar has been popular all over the world.

4 The USB typewriter can be attached to any computer.

5 The USB typewriter can be transported easily.

6 The USB typewriter was made in the USA.

Articles

Politics | Obits | Education | Earth | Science | Defence | Health | Art

Necessary or just fun?

There are many strange things available to buy on the internet. But how useful are they? If you've bought something strange, did you find you needed it or has it never been used? Here are two things that might fit either category.

First, the UFO cookie jar. It is shaped like a spaceship with an alien sitting on top. The alien's eyes light up to frighten anyone who is tempted to open the jar. Once the biscuits have been placed in the jar, they are protected from anyone trying to lose weight but who tries to get a biscuit secretly! Any type of biscuit can be stored in the jar and the unusual design makes it a talking point.

Second, a 'back to the future' gadget! Typewriters may be things of the past but this invention means they can be brought back. It's the USB typewriter and it can be plugged into any computer with a USB port. It then becomes the computer's keyboard and is equipped with all the functions of a normal keyboard, although obviously it can't be carried around like a laptop! The typewriter was made in the USA.

3 **Find and underline 11 passive verb forms in the article.**

4 **Rewrite the sentences in the active voice.**

1 Advertisements are seen by many people before they buy a product.

2 Spring and summer fashions are presented by their designers in Fashion Weeks in London, Paris and Milan.

3 Models are helped with their make-up and hair by make-up artists and hair stylists.

4 The jewels were put on sale last week by the person who stole them.

5 The spring collection was designed by a famous Italian model.

6 This jacket has already been worn by somebody else.

5 **Complete the second sentence so that it means the same as the first. Use no more than three words.**

1 People often advertise things they don't want on the internet.

Unwanted things _____ on the internet.

2 Apparently, somebody buys a mobile phone every six seconds on that website.

Apparently, a mobile phone _____ every six seconds on that website.

3 It's important to check the security of a site if you want to buy something on the internet.

It's important that the security of a site _____ if you want to buy something on the internet.

4 They sold 12,000 tickets online.

12,000 tickets _____ online.

5 People find good deals on cars on the internet.

Good deals on cars _____ on the internet.

6 They sold this antique teapot to the highest bidder.

This antique teapot _____ to the highest bidder.

7 They've pulled down those old shops in the High Street to make space for a shopping centre.

Those old shops in the High Street _____ down to make space for a shopping centre.

8 They gave the owners some money as compensation.

The owners _____ some money as compensation.

9 People sometimes make mistakes and don't like something they've bought.

Mistakes _____ by people who don't like something they've bought.

10 Once I nearly bought a car that the owner was advertising for £5!

Once I nearly bought a car that _____ for £5!

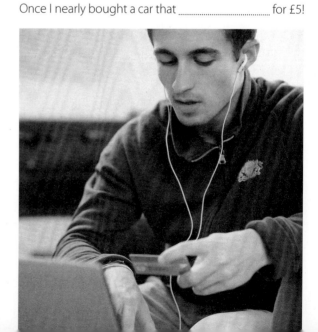

Vocabulary

shops and services ▶ CB page 88

1 Match products 1–8 with shops A–H.

1	sofa	A	chemist's
2	dictionary	B	bookshop
3	cough medicine	C	greengrocer's
4	sausages	D	butcher's
5	plants	E	shoe shop
6	boots	F	jeweller's
7	bracelet	G	furniture store
8	vegetables	H	florist's

2 Identify these shops not mentioned in Activity 1.

1 I buy all my clothes in a small b..................... – I don't like big chain stores.

2 I spend all my time in my local c.................. s..................! My laptop's always going wrong!

3 I get fresh bread from the b..................... every morning.

4 My local n..................... sells sweets and other things, as well as papers and magazines.

5 The s..................... outside my town is huge. It sells almost everything, including petrol.

6 I like shopping in d..................... s..................... because I can buy so many different things in one place.

3 ▶ 35 Listen and match each speaker (1–8) with a shop from Activities 1 and 2.

1	....	4	....	7	....
2	....	5	....	8	....
3	....	6	....		

4 Listen again and match each speaker (1–8) with replies A–H below.

A Oh, now we're here let's do our shopping – it might be better by the time we've finished.

B We have a good choice here. What colour are you interested in?

C Of course. Would you like it sliced?

D Certainly. These are on special offer today – and they're very tasty.

E I have these painkillers but you need to see a dentist!

F Which operating system are you using?

G Just a minute and I'll measure your finger.

H Would you like red ones or a mix of red and white?

5 ▶ 36 Listen and check your answers to Activity 4.

Grammar

get/have something done ▶ CB page 89

1 Rewrite the sentences using the correct form of *have something done*.

1 The hairdresser cut my hair last week.
I .... last week.

2 Some painters are repainting our building next week.
We .... next week.

3 A dressmaker is mending Julio's jeans.
Julio .... by a dressmaker.

4 A manicurist painted Jana's toenails bright green.
Jana .... by a manicurist.

5 A cleaner is cleaning our windows at the moment.
We .... at the moment.

6 A friend fixed my computer.
I .... by a friend.

7 A shoemaker in Italy makes my friend's shoes by hand.
My friend .... by hand in Italy.

8 A local mechanic always repairs my car.
I always .... by a local mechanic.

2 Put the words in the correct order to make questions.

1 get / your / where / hair / do / cut / you / ?

2 car / often / serviced / how / get / you / do / your / ?

3 why / tattoo / done / get / did / you / a / ?

4 old / how / your / were / when / ears / pierced / you / got / you / ?

5 teeth / whitened / when / get / your / did / you / ?

6 shirt / made / get / you / did / that / where / ?

7 often / how / your / you / get / eyes / do / tested / ?

8 did / she / portrait / when / her / painted / have / ?

3 ▶ 37 Match the questions in Activity 2 with answers A–H below. Then listen and check.

A Last month. I brush them well now to keep them looking good.

B I bought it online.

C I don't know. I just thought it looked good.

D I haven't had them pierced yet.

E Once a year, otherwise I think it's not safe to drive.

F Every year – I think it's a good thing to do.

G At the barber shop on the corner. Do you like it?

H Last week. The artist was Italian, I think.

Reading

Multiple choice (Part 1) ▶ CB page 90

About the exam:
In this part of the exam you read five short texts. They may be signs, notices, labels, notes or messages. Each one has three different explanations (A, B, C). You choose the option that explains the meaning of the sign.

Strategy:
- Look at the text. Think about where you might see it and what it means.
- Read the three options carefully and decide which one is closest in meaning to the text.
- Check the other options to make sure they are wrong.

1 Look at the text in each question. What does it say? Choose the correct option, A–C.

1

> **15% discount for students who show a valid student card**

A Students must use a card to buy something.
B Cards used to buy something must be valid.
C If students show their card, they pay less money.

2

> **Longer opening hours during our summer sale period**

A The shop is open for more time all the summer.
B There are more things for sale during the summer.
C People have more time to buy things during the summer sales.

3

> THE TOILETS ON THE THIRD FLOOR ARE CLOSED FOR **MAINTENANCE**. THERE ARE NEW **FACILITIES** FOR CUSTOMERS ON THE FOURTH FLOOR.

A No one can use the toilets on the third floor.
B Customers can choose whether to use the toilets on the third or fourth floor.
C All the toilets are being improved.

4

> All sale items are returnable within seven days as long as the **receipt** is shown.

A You can return any sale items at any time with a receipt.
B Sale items can only be returned if the customer has the receipt.
C Receipts are only valid for seven days.

5

> Mum, I'm still having trouble with my new laptop – it needs checking over. Can you take it back to the computer store on Saturday, please? They shouldn't **charge** anything as it's new.

The boy wants his mother to
A return the laptop to the store for repair.
B ask the store for a refund.
C collect a new laptop from the store.

2 Match the words in bold in Activity 1 with definitions 1–6.

1 a piece of paper which shows how much you have paid for something
2 ask someone to pay a particular amount of money for something
3 an amount of time
4 keeping something working correctly
5 correct and usable; not out-of-date
6 rooms or services that are available in a place

3 Complete the sentences with words from Activity 2.

1 The service in the hotel wasn't very good but the .... were fantastic. There was a huge pool, a spa and a fully-equipped gym.
2 The computer shop didn't .... me any extra money for transferring data onto my new laptop.
3 The .... work on the facilities in the shopping centre is taking a long time.
4 Is your passport still ....? Mine has expired.
5 I can't take that hairdryer back to the shop because I've lost the ....
6 He visited the UK 20 times over a .... of five years.

Vocabulary

verbs and prepositions ▶ CB page 91

1 **Choose the correct alternative in each sentence.**

1 Have you heard *about* / *on* that new department store in town?

2 I'm looking *into* / *for* some new shoes to wear to the party on Saturday.

3 The shop assistant apologised *about* / *for* the slow service.

4 On the internet you can choose *from* / *in* a wide variety of products.

5 I hate complaining *about* / *with* poor service but sometimes you just have to!

6 I insist *on* / *in* seeing the whole menu before choosing food.

7 I never succeed *about* / *in* getting discounts – I'm not good at bargaining!

8 I spent a lot of time searching *on* / *for* the right presents for my friends.

2 **Find and correct the mistakes with prepositions in the sentences.**

1 I'm planning for go shopping on Saturday.

2 I always listen at my friends when they tell me what clothes suit me.

3 My friend Carla always complains on the bad service in the local restaurant.

4 I hate arguing of anything but sometimes I disagree with my friends.

5 I'm planning to going shopping with friends this weekend.

6 I lent my book for a friend but he lost it.

7 I told my friend for that new shop but she didn't like it.

8 Do you ever argue to friends about money?

3 **Complete the conversation. Use a preposition in each gap.**

Sam: What are you doing in the holidays?

Adam: I'm planning **(1)** .... going on a camping trip with some friends.

Sam: Where are you thinking **(2)** .... going?

Adam: Well, I've been looking **(3)** .... information on the internet and there are loads of places to choose **(4)** .... Have you ever heard anything **(5)** .... camping in Ireland?

Sam: Don't people complain **(6)** .... the weather there? Apparently, it rains a lot.

Adam: Maybe, but it's supposed to be really beautiful and the people are famous **(7)** .... being really friendly. By the way, can I borrow your tent?

Sam: Sorry but I've promised to lend it **(8)** .... my cousin Ana.

Speaking

Simulated situation (Part 2)
▶ CB page 92

1 ▶ **38 Look at the instructions and pictures an examiner gave two candidates. Then listen to what the candidates said and decide if the sentences are true or false.**

> I'm going to describe a situation to you. You have decided to sell some things that you don't use anymore. Talk together about these ways of selling things and decide which would be the best way of selling each of the things you want to sell. Here is a picture with some ideas to help you.

1 The boy is worried about selling things online.

2 The girl has used PayPal.

3 The boy has a PayPal account.

4 The girl thinks Cyberbuy is a better place to sell things than a flea market.

5 The boy decides to sell the books at a flea market.

6 The girl doesn't look at newspaper advertisements and neither does the boy.

7 The boy thinks the painting isn't worth much.

8 The girl agrees that taking the painting to a market could be risky.

2 **Listen again and complete the sentences from the recording.**

1 I .... wouldn't do it on the internet.

2 Do you .... it's too risky?

3 You have to set up an account or ....

4 You could be .... but I think you'd get more money for the things on Cyberbuy.

5 I suppose ...., now I come to think of it.

6 That's a good ....

3 **Find and correct the mistakes in the sentences a candidate copied down when she was listening to the conversation in Activity 2.**

1 If I wanted sell some things, I definitely wouldn't do it on the internet.

2 The goods are usually send after the money has been received.

3 That's what I've be told.

4 You could to be right.

5 It might get damage.

6 That's good point.

7 A friend of my sells paintings on the internet.

8 He make quite a lot of money.

Writing

Note (Part 2) ▶ CB page 93

1 **Look at the exam task, the answers two candidates have written and their teacher's comments. Match the teacher's comments (A–B) with the candidates' answers (1–2).**

You received a gift from an English friend called Patrick. Write a card to your friend. In the card you should:

- thank your friend for the gift.
- say why you like it so much.
- say when you are going to use it.

Write 35–45 words.

1 Dear Patrick,

Thank you much for book. I start read it as soon as I will finish studing to my exams.

Bye for now,

Tania

2 hi patrick i've just opened the parcel with the book you sent i love fantasy novels as you know i've already started reading it it's absolutely fantastic love fabiola

A This is a good message but you have missed one of the points you were asked to cover. There is another problem. You have written this in the form of a text message sent by mobile phone with no punctuation or capital letters.

B This is quite a good message in terms of layout and punctuation but you have missed one of the points you were supposed to cover. There are also some grammar mistakes and one spelling mistake.

2 **Rewrite the candidates' answers from Activity 2, correcting the grammar, punctuation and spelling mistakes.**

3 **Now add an extra sentence in each of the answers so that they both cover all of the points in the exam task.**

4 **Look at this exam task. This time the candidate has answered the question fully but has made several spelling mistakes. Find and correct the mistakes.**

You want to send a gift to your English pen friend, James, because he sent you a book last month but you are not sure what he likes. Write an email to your friend. In your email you should:

- thank him for his gift.
- explain why you want to send a gift.
- ask him what he likes.

Write 35–45 words.

Dear James,

Thank you for sending me the book, wich I enjoied very much. I would like to send you a gift in retern because I was so pleesed. What are your favurite things? Please tell me so I can send you somthing.

Bye,

Carla

5 **Now write your own answer to the exam task in Activity 4.**

A small world

11

Reading

Multiple choice (Part 4) ▶ CB page 96

1 Read the article quickly and decide if this sentence is true or false.

The writer has never travelled to a foreign country.

On the road in a foreign language

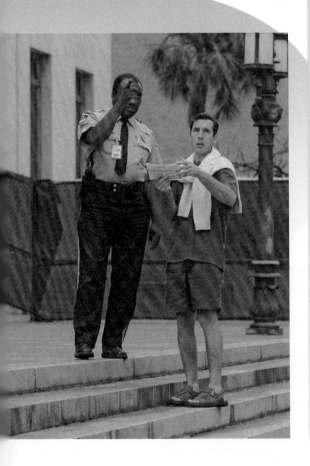

How often have you had the experience of a tourist in your country asking you a question in their language and just expecting you to understand them? How do you feel when this happens? Perhaps you don't have any idea what they're saying and you hurry away in **confusion** and **embarrassment**. Maybe you know the language and feel proud that you are able to respond. If, on the other hand, you're anything like me, you probably feel **irritated** or even a little angry.

When this happens to me, I try to be polite and friendly, of course, even if I don't understand, but it reminds me just how important it is to try and learn the language of the places I visit. I know that I'm **unlikely** to be able to learn much

if I'm only going to be there for a few days rather than a few weeks but I can at least try to learn the things I will almost certainly need to say. I mean **greetings** like 'hello' and 'goodbye', the words for 'please' and 'thank you', how to ask politely for goods or services, how to ask how much they cost and how to ask for directions.

You might be thinking that there's not much point knowing how to ask a question like that if you are not going to be able to understand the reply. Even so, at least you've shown you are willing to make an effort and that often makes all the difference. Perhaps the person you ask will show you where to go or even take you there. If you just ask them in your language, they might not even bother to answer.

2 Read the article in Activity 1 again and these questions. For each question, mark the correct letter A, B, C or D.

1 What is the writer trying to do in this text?

   A complain about foreign tourists

   B admit that he is not good at learning languages

   C tell you what to study when you learn a foreign language

   D persuade travellers that learning languages has benefits

2 How does the author feel when foreign tourists speak to him in their language?

   A pleased

   B confused

   C annoyed

   D ashamed

3 What does the author do if he is only going to visit a country for a short time?

   A He doesn't bother to learn the language.

   B He learns how to say the things that are absolutely necessary.

   C He tries to be polite to people even if he doesn't understand them.

   D He studies the language for a few weeks before he leaves home.

4 Why can knowing only a few words and phrases be a problem?

   A You can't have a proper conversation with anyone.

   B You might get an answer that is too difficult for you to understand.

   C You might look as if you have not tried hard enough to learn the language.

   D You might seem to know more of the language than you actually do.

5 What, according to the writer, might a local person think when a tourist tries to speak the local language?

   A 'I'll try and help them since they've obviously tried to learn my language.'

   B 'Even if I try and answer their question, I don't think they'll understand.'

   C 'I'm in a hurry and I can't waste time trying to talk to these people.'

   D 'They should learn my language properly if they want to try and speak it.'

3 Complete the sentences with words formed from the words in bold in the text.

1 I'm _____! What do we have to do here?

2 I've never been so _____ in my life! I went bright red.

3 I find it really _____ when people talk in loud voices on their mobile phones.

4 It's _____ to rain later. Take an umbrella.

5 The new teacher _____ the class and told us her name.

Vocabulary

compound adjectives ▶ CB page 97

1 Match 1–8 with A–H to make compound adjectives.

1	one-	**A**	made
2	self-	**B**	fashioned
3	energy-	**C**	way
4	hand-	**D**	lit
5	old-	**E**	minute
6	world-	**F**	service
7	brightly-	**G**	famous
8	20-	**H**	efficient

2 Complete the compound adjectives with the words in the box.

age   assured   confident   paid   painted
sewn   time   written

1 old-_____, old-_____

2 self-_____, self-_____

3 hand-_____, hand-_____

4 well-/badly-_____, well-/badly-_____

3 Complete the sentences with compound adjectives from Activities 1 and 2.

1 I can't imagine being an _____ pensioner – I'm too young!

2 I hate eating in _____ restaurants on holiday. I prefer to have a waiter who brings me my food.

3 I'd love to buy a _____ ticket to Australia and never come back.

4 I like to buy _____ pictures of places I visit. They are much nicer than mass-produced souvenirs.

5 My aim in life is to have a _____ job so that I have plenty of money.

travel and transport ▶ CB page 98

4 Find seven words in the wordsearch connected with travel. Five of the words are in plural form.

j	m	p	g	t	h	s	o	u	v	e	n	i	r	s	e
w	c	a	p	a	t	o	s	q	b	k	c	e	w	j	w
d	w	h	p	h	o	v	l	x	a	y	g	n	a	o	i
e	k	q	g	s	o	m	m	i	p	e	j	r	a	u	k
s	r	i	n	e	p	u	o	s	d	m	l	u	x	r	j
p	l	h	o	t	e	l	s	q	q	a	a	o	m	n	m
f	d	o	l	v	b	y	v	b	k	h	y	j	z	e	p
g	u	i	d	e	b	o	o	k	s	n	h	i	x	y	x

5 Complete the article with words from the wordsearch in Activity 4.

How did we all live without apps?

More than 160 million smartphones or app-compatible devices are owned worldwide, and over ten billion apps have been downloaded onto them. These include more than 17,000 apps for travellers. What they do is help you find information quickly and easily while you're moving around. Once you have found the cheapest **(1)** f................... to get you to your destination, you can book five star **(2)** h................... to stay in, and even talk into an app that translates your words instantly – though you do have to speak very clearly to avoid misunderstandings!

Here are three free apps that travellers can't seem to manage without:

World at your Feet
This includes information published in good **(3)** g................... so you can check out all you need to know before setting off on your **(4)** j.................... There is advice on where to stay, buy **(5)** s................... to take home and find the best bargains. One big plus is the currency converter that tells you the best exchange rate.

Skiing International
See current conditions on live webcams set up on the tops of mountains. Skiers can also pass on up-to-date news about the slopes. There are satellite images and weather **(6)** m................... so you won't end up in a snowstorm!

On the Road Pics
Take photographs and then add notes on the screen before you upload them to your social networking site or email them to friends. It turns your **(7)** h................... into a travel story!

6 Read the article in Activity 5 again and complete these sentences.

1 The advantage of the *World at your Feet* app is that you always know the best ....
....

2 *Skiing International* provides information from .... and skiers.

3 *On the Road Pics* means you can ....
.... to share with other people.

phrasal verbs of travel
▶ CB page 98

7 Read the sentences and match the phrasal verbs (1–4) with the patterns (A–D).

1 I love **catching up with** news about my friends on email.

2 I usually **pick** my friend **up** from the station when she comes to visit me.

3 I often **set off** on holiday on a Friday night because there's less traffic.

4 It's always a good idea to **look for** cheap flights on the internet.

A verb with no object
B verb + preposition + object
C verb + object + preposition
D verb + preposition + preposition

8 Replace the underlined verb in each sentence with the correct form of a phrasal verb from the box.

end up	get rid of	look for	set off
set up	turn into		

1 I hate <u>starting</u> on a journey early in the morning – I'm never awake!

2 On one holiday I got lost and <u>found myself</u> in a forest!

3 I <u>try to find</u> cheap hotels but they are often not very good.

4 I never <u>throw away</u> old photographs – they hold happy memories.

5 It's useful when people <u>place</u> webcams in different locations – it's easy to find out about the weather.

6 My last holiday <u>became</u> an absolute nightmare – everything went wrong!

Listening

Multiple choice (Part 1) ▶ CB page 99

1 ▶ 39 **Listen to the recording. For each question, choose the correct picture and put a tick (✓) in the box below it.**

1 Which activity does the girl decide to do?

A ☐   B ☐   C ☐

2 Which photograph are they talking about?

A ☐   B ☐   C ☐

3 When will the new leisure centre open officially?

A ☐   B ☐   C ☐

4 How will the family travel to their holiday destination this year?

A ☐   B ☐   C ☐

5 What does the man decide to eat for lunch?

A ☐   B ☐   C ☐

6 What did the girl like best about being on holiday?

A ☐   B ☐   C ☐

7 When will the plane take off?

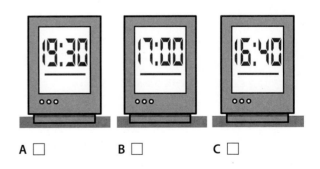

A ☐   B ☐   C ☐

Grammar

future forms ▶ CB page 100

1 **Complete the conversations with the correct future forms.**

1 **A:** I don't think Georgina .... (*get on*) with Ryan. They're too different from one another.

   B: I don't know about that. I'm sure she .... (*like*) him.

2 **A:** Where .... (*you/meet*) Chrysa?

   B: Outside the main post office in Athens.

   A: When?

   B: We .... (*meet*) at 1.30 and .... (*have*) lunch with some friends of hers.

3 **A:** What shall we get Ahmed's mother? We .... (*have to*) give her something since she's invited us to stay.

   B: We could get her something typical from here.

   A: I know! I .... (*get*) her some of those earrings we saw and you can buy her a matching bracelet.

4 **A:** What are your plans for the future?

   B: I .... (*study*) tourism but before that I .... (*take*) six months off to travel. I .... (*visit*) some relatives in Australia.

2 **Choose the correct alternative in each sentence.**

1 What *do you do / are you going to do* this summer?

2 What time *does your plane leave / will your plane leave*?

3 Look at those huge dark clouds. It looks like it *rains / is going to rain* later.

4 Next Monday *I have / I'll have* a French lesson in the evening. After that *I probably study / I'll probably study* for the test on Wednesday.

5 '*Are you having / Do you have* a dessert?' 'No, *I just have / I'm just going to have* a coffee.'

6 The meeting *starts / is starting* at 8.00 – let's meet at the station at 7.15.

7 'What *do you do / are you going to do* with all this paint?' 'Paint my bedroom!'

8 *I'll have / I'm having* lunch with Pete tomorrow. We *meet / are meeting* at Wendy's Diner at noon. Would you like to join us?

9 What time *does the lesson start / is the lesson starting*?

10 I'm sure *you'll have / you're having* a great time at Lee's party on Saturday.

Speaking

Extended turn (Part 3) ▶ CB page 101

1 ▶ **40** **Listen to what an examiner asked two candidates to do and to their replies. Which photograph does each candidate describe?**

2 **Listen again and decide if these sentences are true or false.**

1 Both candidates summarise the content of the photo at the beginning.

2 Only Yasmina describes the different parts of the photo in detail.

3 Only Fatima uses a lot of different adjectives.

4 Both candidates use prepositions of place.

3 **Listen again and note down the prepositions of place the candidates use.**

4 **Write a description of the third photo in Activity 1.**

Grammar

will and *going to* ▶ CB page 102

1 **Complete the conversation with the correct form of *going to* or *will*.**

Bojena: You **(1)** .... be pleased to hear that I **(2)** .... get a dog.

Darko: At last! I'm sure you **(3)** .... be glad you did. You **(4)** .... be able to take him for walks. Have you decided what kind you **(5)** .... get?

Bojena: Well, I've been looking at some websites on dogs and I can't make up my mind. I think it **(6)** .... be either a cocker spaniel or a golden retriever.

Darko: When **(7)** .... buy it?

Bojena: I **(8)** .... (*not*) buy one, actually. I **(9)** .... get a dog from an animal refuge. Do you want to come with me? Maybe you **(10)** .... find a friend for Eddie.

2 **Find and correct the mistakes with *will* and *going to* in the sentences. Tick (✓) the sentences that are correct.**

1 You can't carry those heavy boxes on your own. I'm going to help you with them.

2 I can see you're very busy. I'll come back later.

3 Naira has decided that she will not get a dog after all.

4 Alberto bought those new jeans. He'll wear them to the party tonight.

5 'Do you want to share a pizza?' 'I think I'll just have a salad, actually.'

6 I don't feel very well. I think I'll go and lie down for a minute.

7 Pablo made an appointment at the hairdresser's. He'll have his hair cut.

8 In ten years' time most of my friends will be married.

Writing

Informal letter (Part 3) ▶ CB page 103

1 **Look at the exam task. What do you have to do?**

A Describe a place in your country and say why your friend should visit it.

B Suggest a place your friend should describe and mention something that has changed there.

> This is part of a letter you receive from your English friend, Daphne, asking for your advice.
>
> *I have to write about a place in your country that has changed recently for a travel web page. What do you think I should write about? What has changed there?*
>
> Now write a letter to your friend answering her questions.
>
> Write a letter in about 100 words.

2 **Look at the letter a candidate wrote. In some places he has used very formal language. His teacher has underlined these parts of the letter. Replace them with the informal expressions in the box.**

all the best   at first   but   let me know   too
you know how

Hi Daphne,

Thanks for your letter. I've been thinking about ① which place you should describe. <u>Initially</u>, I thought you could write about London.

② <u>I am sure you are aware of the way</u> it's always changing, especially with the Olympics and everything. The trouble is everyone writes about London.

Well, I've had another idea. Why don't you write about Sheffield? Some people complain about ③ the city council. <u>However</u>, they've banned cars in the centre of the city, which is a big improvement, in my opinion. They've started ④ organising all sorts of cultural events <u>as well</u>. Last month there was even a Moroccan craft market!

Well, I'd better finish this letter and get to bed. ⑤ <u>I look forward to hearing</u> how you get on.

⑥ <u>Yours sincerely</u>,

Nilo

3 **Write your answer to Daphne's letter.**

Extreme

Grammar

zero and first conditionals ▶ CB page 105

1 Match the first half of the zero conditional sentences (1–6) with the second (A–F).

1	When people eat the wrong type of food,	**A**	it cries.
2	If you heat ice,	**B**	they stay healthy.
3	When a baby is hungry,	**C**	they get ill.
4	If people take regular exercise,	**D**	they get hurt.
5	If people go out in the rain,	**E**	it melts.
6	Unless people take care on mountains,	**F**	they get wet.

2 Write a zero conditional sentence with *if* for each pair of sentences.

1 I don't have anything to do on Saturday mornings. I have breakfast in a café.
2 I have a match. I have something quick at home.
3 I walk to the park. It's a nice day.
4 It's raining. My friend drives me.
5 The coach tells us off for playing badly. We lose.
6 We win. He takes us all out for a pizza.

3 Find and correct the mistakes in the sentences.

1 You'll never swim fast if you practise a lot.
2 I tell you if I decide to take that climbing course.
3 If we'll miss the last train, we'll have to walk home.
4 Unless you will work hard, you won't be successful.
5 You feel very proud if you get to the top of the mountain.
6 If you ask me to do something, I do it for you.

4 Match the first half of the first conditional sentences (1–6) with the second (A–F).

1 I'll watch television tonight
2 If he doesn't win the competition,
3 Unless I get a taxi quickly,
4 I'll have to buy an umbrella
5 When he hears what she said, he'll be angry
6 If my computer crashes again,

A unless she apologises.
B I'll be late for the meeting.
C he'll be very disappointed.
D I'll get really annoyed with it!
E if there's anything interesting on.
F if it doesn't stop raining.

5 Complete the article with the correct form of the verbs in the box.

change	get (x2)	look	respond	roll
speak	stop	treat		

The lion whisperer

What do you think a lion will do if you walk up to it and kiss it on the nose? Have you for breakfast or purr like a pussycat? According to animal behaviourist Kevin Richardson, if you **(1)** .... down to the lion's level, **(2)** .... into its eyes and **(3)** .... softly, it **(4)** .... over and go to sleep. What's more, Richardson, who is also known as the 'lion whisperer', gets so friendly with the lions he works with he can actually sleep with them.

But what will happen if the lion **(5)** .... hungry during the night? Will you become his next snack? Not at all, apparently. Kevin says that if you **(6)** .... lions with respect, they **(7)** .... with respect, affection and even love. He thinks we've been getting it wrong with animals like lions. Perhaps if we **(8)** .... trying to dominate them, they **(9)** .... their attitudes to humans and begin to see us as friends.

Listening
True/False (Part 4) ▶ CB page 105

1 ▶ 41 **You will hear a conversation between two friends, Sara and Michael, about a television programme called *Special Talents*. Listen and decide if each sentence is correct or incorrect. If it is correct, put a tick (✓) in the box under A for YES. If it is incorrect, put a tick (✓) in the box under B for NO.**

                                                                           A   B

1 Sara was impressed because people in the programme were not proud of themselves.   ☐   ☐

2 Michael doesn't believe that everyone has different natural abilities.   ☐   ☐

3 Sara finds it difficult to believe that Beethoven had physical problems.   ☐   ☐

4 Michael believes that running fast is something anyone can do if they practise.   ☐   ☐

5 Sara suggests that even talented people must have help.   ☐   ☐

6 Michael suggests that there is a difference between ability and talent.   ☐   ☐

2 **Complete the sentences with the correct verb forms. Use the verbs in brackets.**

1 If talented people .... (*not get*) any encouragement, they often .... (*give up*).

2 I .... (*get*) very discouraged if people .... (*criticise*) me.

3 If I .... (*manage*) to teach my dog Dixie to do some new tricks, we .... (*go*) on *Britain's Got Talent*.

4 Who .... (*you/talk*) to when you .... (*be*) worried about something?

5 Where .... (*you/go*) when you .... (*want*) to meet people of your own age?

6 I'm going on holiday next week. If the weather .... (*be*) good, I .... (*spend*) all the time on the beach.

7 I want to learn how to rock climb. If I .... (*do*), I .... (*climb*) a mountain in Scotland next summer.

8 How .... (*you/feel*) when you .... (*not get*) enough sleep?

9 I'm going skiing for the first time and I'm looking forward to it. But if weather conditions .... (*be*) too difficult, I .... (*give up*) and come home.

10 Unless it .... (*stop*) raining soon, I .... (*not go out*) this afternoon.

Reading

Multiple choice (Part 1) ▶ CB page 106

1 **Choose the sentence that best describes the meaning of the first sentence.**

1 Sharp bend ahead!
  A Be careful because there is a dangerous corner in front of you.
  B Always look in front of you when there is a dangerous corner.

2 This door is alarmed.
  A Opening the door will set off the alarm.
  B Please ring the alarm before opening the door.

3 In case of fire, use the stairs.
  A Use the stairs in case there is a fire.
  B Use the stairs when there is a fire.

4 Don't leave your bag unattended in the airport.
  A Keep your bag with you at all times in the airport.
  B Leave your bag with an attendant, not in the airport.

5 Leave the building immediately if the fire alarm goes off.
  A Stay in the building unless there is a fire.
  B Don't stay in the building if the fire alarm sounds.

2 **Look at the text in each question. What does it say? Choose the correct option, A–C.**

1

> This film contains extreme scenes that may be **unsuitable** for children under 12.

  A Children under 12 are not allowed to see this film.
  B This film is not **recommended** for children under 12.
  C This film has scenes with children under 12.

2

DANGER: CLEANER AT WORK. FLOOR MAY BE WET.

  A Take care because you may fall.
  B The cleaner may be doing **dangerous** work.
  C If you make the floor wet, the cleaner will come.

3

> **STAND BEHIND THE YELLOW LINES WHEN A TRAIN IS APPROACHING.**

  A Do not cross the yellow lines if a train is coming.
  B Passengers should always wait for trains behind the yellow lines.
  C There is danger behind the yellow lines if a train is coming.

4

> **To:** Mr Jackson
> **From:** Climbing International
>
> **Unfortunately**, bad weather conditions are continuing to cause avalanches high on the mountain so the expedition has been postponed for at least a week.

The email from Climbing International
  A warns Mr Jackson not to go on the expedition.
  B explains why the expedition has been **delayed**.
  C rearranges the expedition for a date in the future.

5

> **EXTREME ACTIVITY DAY**
> AT WESTFIELD PARK, SATURDAY 15 MAY
> Tickets available on the gate or in advance with 10% discount. Everyone **welcome** but you must be over 18 to do parachuting.

The advert says that the activity day
  A can be fun for all the family.
  B is cheaper if you buy tickets before 15 May.
  C has some activities that are for children.

3 **Complete the sentences with a word in bold from Activity 2. There is one word you do not need to use.**

1 Of course you can bring your dog. Pets are always .... here!
2 Our plane was .... for two hours because of a technical problem.
3 The train is now .... its final destination.
4 We asked the hotel receptionist and she .... a restaurant where they serve fresh fish.
5 ...., we won't be able to join you.
6 Everyone knows that lions are very .... animals.

Vocabulary

confusing words ▶ CB page 107

1 **Choose the correct alternative in each sentence.**

1 I never *remember / remind* my friends' birthdays – it's very embarrassing!

2 Here, *bring / take* this with you – you might need it.

3 It's great to go on day *trips / travels* with my family.

4 Please *bring / take* your homework to the next class so that I can mark it.

5 I often need *remembering / reminding* about work I have to finish.

6 Would you like to *come / go* to my house and have dinner with me tonight?

7 Let's *come / go* to the cinema on Saturday.

8 I find that *travel / trip* is often very tiring.

2 **Choose from the pairs of words in the box to complete the sentences. You may need to change the form of some words.**

learn/teach   lend/borrow   live/stay   lose/miss
work/job

1 I'd love to _____ for a company in another country one day.

2 It's often a mistake to _____ money to friends – it can cause problems.

3 If I _____ the eight o'clock bus, I get to work late.

4 When I'm travelling, I love to _____ in small family-run hotels.

5 I'm terrible with small objects – I keep _____ my car keys!

6 I'd love to _____ in a home in an extreme climate – it must be exciting.

7 Being a ski instructor is my ideal _____ .

8 I think that it's very hard to _____ another language quickly.

9 It's getting more and more difficult to _____ money from a bank nowadays.

10 It must be fun to _____ people to ski – I'd love to do that!

Grammar

second conditional ▶ CB page 108

1 **Find and correct the mistakes in the sentences. Tick (✓) the sentences that are correct.**

1 If I were bitten by a poisonous spider, I will go straight to the hospital.

2 If I see a big vicious dog coming towards me, I would run away.

3 If I were lost in a forest, I would stay where I was and wait for help.

4 If a friend of mine fell into the water, I would cover them with a blanket.

5 If I saw a shark while I was swimming, I will try to swim away.

6 If a bear comes up to me while I was hiking in the woods, I would try to frighten it away.

2 **Complete the sentences with the correct form of the verbs in the box.**

hit   lie   put   stand   tell   walk

A I wouldn't. I _____ downhill.

B I wouldn't. I _____ face down and keep still.

C I would too but I _____ them to take their wet clothes off first.

D I wouldn't. I _____ still and look away.

E I wouldn't. I _____ it on the nose.

F I would too but I _____ some ice on the bite first.

3 **Match the sentences in Activity 1 with the responses in Activity 2.**

4 **Match the responses in Activity 2 with these reasons.**

1 It might lose interest and go away.

2 They wouldn't get warm quickly enough otherwise.

3 It would stop the poison spreading.

4 It might frighten it away.

5 They just get more aggressive if you make eye contact with them.

6 You are more likely to find a river or stream there.

5 Complete the blog entry about extreme sports. Use one word in each gap.

Indoor skydiving

Ever wondered what it **(1)** .... be like if you **(2)** .... fly like a bird? Indoor skydiving centres have vertical wind tunnels that let you experience what the world **(3)** .... be like if there **(4)** .... no gravity. And what **(5)** .... it be like? Well, you **(6)** .... be able to fly for one thing. Before you start real skydiving, try the indoor version. It's amazing!

Speaking

Simulated situation (Part 2) ▶ CB page 109

1 ▶ 42 **Look at the exam task below and an examiner's comments about two candidates, Maria and Petros, on the right. Listen and match the candidates with the comments. Write *M* for *Maria* or *P* for *Petros*.**

I'm going to describe a situation to you. You are going on an expedition in an area a long way from the nearest town or city. You need to add two things to the survival kit you have already prepared. Talk together about the different things you could add and decide which ones would be most useful in an emergency. Here is a picture with some ideas to help you.

1 *Grammar: good in general. A few mistakes with conditional sentences.* ....

2 *Vocabulary: used some excellent vocabulary.* ....

3 *Organisation of ideas: not so good. Started with one idea and then switched to another. Didn't always give reasons for choices.* ....

4 *Communication with partner: didn't really try to involve the other candidate or respond to suggestions.* ....

2 **Here are the incorrect conditional sentences the examiner mentioned. Find and correct the mistakes.**

1 You can eat the chocolate bar if you were hungry.

2 If the cigarette lighter didn't work, the candle had not been any good.

3 We don't have any time to draw pictures if we were lost!

3 **Complete the correct conditional sentences the other candidate used.**

1 If you .... lost for several days, you .... get very hungry.

2 And then you'd .... nothing to eat if you .... lost.

3 If someone .... a cut or scratch, we .... need to clean the wound.

4 If they .... out a search party for us, they .... be able to see where we had been.

4 **Listen again and check your answers to Activity 3.**

Vocabulary

sport and leisure ▶ CB page 110

1 **Match verbs 1–10 with nouns A–J to make collocations connected with different sports.**

1	kick	A	a goal
2	row	B	a sport
3	throw	C	a football
4	run	D	a competition
5	enter	E	a bike
6	practise	F	a marathon
7	hit	G	a javelin
8	score	H	a tennis ball
9	ride	I	a hockey ball
10	serve	J	a boat

2 ▶ 43 **Listen to four people talking about their sport. Match each speaker (1–4) with a sport from the box. There are two you do not need to use.**

athletics	cycling	football	hiking	surfing
tennis				

1 .... 2 .... 3 .... 4 ....

3 **Some candidates have completed these sentences about sport and leisure with the words from the box. In some cases they have chosen the wrong words. Find and correct the mistakes. Tick (✓) the words that are correct.**

compete	enter	experienced	fitness
instructor	join in	practice	prize	safety
train			

1 Tobias has decided to join in a surfing competition next month but he doesn't expect to win a prize.

2 She's a wonderful instructor. She always shows us what to do and encourages the shy, less confident members of the group to enter too.

3 Kim has started to compete for the marathon next year. She runs a couple of kilometres every day and does exercises to develop her overall safety.

4 If you are not an experienced climber, you need to use a lot of fitness equipment.

5 I haven't had enough practice rollerblading to train against other people in races or competitions.

do, go, play ▶ CB page 110

4 **Complete the sentences with the correct form of *do, go* or *play*.**

1 I .... athletics when I was at school.

2 Have you ever .... baseball? It's a great game.

3 My grandfather .... dancing at a local club a couple of times a month.

4 A lot of young people .... golf nowadays. It's become quite fashionable.

5 We all had to .... gymnastics when I was at school. Some students loved it but a few of us hated it.

6 My sister cracked a tooth when she was .... hockey. She got hit in the mouth by the ball.

7 Let's .... horse-riding next weekend.

8 A lot of people wear headphones and listen to music whenever they .... jogging.

9 Tina's been .... karate for six months now.

10 Rugby is a very rough game and people often get hurt when they .... it.

11 We were going to .... sailing but the weather forecast said there would be a storm.

12 My grandmother has been .... yoga all her adult life. She's incredibly flexible.

Writing

Sentence transformations (Part 1)
▶ CB page 111

1 **Here are some sentences about the Olympic Games. Complete the second sentence so that it means the same as the first. Use no more than three words.**

1 The Olympic Games take place every four years.
There are four years .... each Olympic Games.

2 No sporting event is as famous as the Olympic Games.
The Olympic Games is .... famous sporting event in the world.

3 Athletes come from all over the world in order to compete in the games.
Athletes come from all over the world .... they can compete in the games.

4 Athletes want to win a gold medal in their event before they go home.
Athletes don't want to go home without .... a gold medal in their event.

5 Some exceptional athletes win several gold medals.
Some exceptional athletes win .... one gold medal.

Vocabulary bank

Using a dictionary

What's in a dictionary?

A dictionary does not just tell you the definition of a word. It also gives you the information you need in order to be able to put the word into a sentence, how to spell it and how to pronounce it.

1 Match the different parts of the dictionary entry (1–8) with their explanations (A–H).

learn /lɜːn || lɜːrn/ *v* past tense and past participle **learned** or **learnt** / lɜːnt || lɜːrnt / *especially BrE*
1 [I,T] to get knowledge of a subject or skill by studying, doing it, or being taught: *What's the best way to learn a language?* | **learn (how) to do sth** *I learned to drive when I was 17.* | **learn (sth) from sb/sth** *I learnt a lot from my father.*

A an example sentence that shows how the word is used
B the pronunciation of the word in both British English and American English
C what prepositions you need and how you use the word with an object or other verb
D extra information about the word such as past forms, plural forms, whether it is countable or uncountable (for a noun), etc.
E the word
F the definition of the word
G the type of word it is
H whether the word (a verb) is transitive (= needs an object) or intransitive (= does not need an object)

understanding pronunciation

At the beginning of a dictionary you can find a list of phonemic symbols with example words which can help you to work out the pronunciation of a word. Word stress is shown by a ' symbol. This symbol appears just before the stressed syllable.

2 Which word is represented by the phonemic symbols?

1 /ɪmˈpɔːtənt/   *important / impossible*
2 /tʃɔɪs/   *choice / choose*
3 /ˈlɪtl/   *later / little*
4 /ɪkˈsept/   *expect / except*
5 /ˈrekɔːd/   *record (n) / record (v)*

knowing a word

3 **Look at the dictionary entry and answer the questions.**

> **include** /in'klu:d/ *v* [T]
> **1** If one thing includes another, the second thing is part of the first: *The price includes lunch.* | **be included in sth** *Service is included in the bill.*
> **2** to allow someone to be part of a group or activity [≠ **exclude**]: *The other children refused to include her in their games.*

1   How is the word spelt?

2   What kind of word is it?

3   Does it need an object?

4   How many different meanings does the word have?

5   What is the opposite of the word?

6   What preposition comes after the word?

7   Does the word have a short or long second vowel?

8   Is the stress of the word on the first or second syllable?

9   *A taxi to the airport is included in the cost of your trip.* Is the word used correctly in this sentence?

10 *When I sent out the invitations, I forgot to include. Sorry about that!* Is the word used correctly in this sentence?

recording a word

4 **Think about the record you keep of new vocabulary and answer the questions.**

1   Which items from the dictionary entries above do you include in your vocabulary records?

2   Which of these items do you think you should keep a record of? Why?

3   How often do you look at your vocabulary records? What do you do to try to learn some of those words? Which techniques work best for you?

It is important to keep good vocabulary notes so that they can help you to understand the meaning and how to use the word in future. Use your notes for revision but make sure you do more than just look at the notes. Try some of these things:

*   Think about the meaning of the word. Is it positive or negative?

*   Think about what words go together with this word.

*   Group words in your list together, e.g. synonyms, same sound, same type of word.

*   Try to connect to the word personally. Do you like it? Does it remind you of anything/anybody?

*   Try to use the word in a sentence. Or try to use five words in a paragraph.

Collocations

prepositional phrases

1 **Write the prepositions in the box in the correct place to complete the table.**

at   by   for   in   on   out of

1	board foot fire purpose time	**4**	date order sight stock work
2	fact a hurry pieces private/public stock	**5**	accident car hand mistake name
3	all last least present the same time	**6**	example instance a long time ever a reason

2 **Complete the sentences with a word or phrase from Activity 1.**

1   The plate was in .... on the kitchen floor. Perhaps the cat had knocked it off the table.

2   I'm afraid these shoes are out of........................ We have a delivery tomorrow so they should be in .... then.

3   Please make sure you come to class on .... tomorrow. Don't be late.

4   Can I speak to you in ...., please? I don't want other people to hear.

5   She was very rude to him but at .... she apologised the next day.

6   My daughter watches TV and chats to her friends online at ....

7   My computer's broken so I've got to write my homework out by ....

8   The coffee machine's out of .... Hopefully, it'll be fixed tomorrow.

9   My car was in the garage on Tuesday so I came to class on ....

10 There were more than 300 passengers on .... the plane.

11 I haven't seen my friend for .... so I'm really looking forward to her visit.

12 I think that everything in life happens for ....

adjectives and prepositions

3 **Write the prepositions in the box in the correct place to complete the table.**

about	at	for	of	to	with

1	4
afraid fond jealous proud tired	famous grateful late responsible suitable
2 confident curious happy sure worried	**5** familiar kind married polite similar
3 good bad brilliant clever terrible	**6** angry bored happy satisfied upset

4 **Complete the sentences with an adjective and preposition from Activity 3.**

1 Kevin is .... maths. He started a maths degree when he was just 14!

2 My best friend met Justin Bieber. I'm so .... her! Why wasn't it me?

3 I'm .... my job these days. I'd like to do something more interesting.

4 This toy isn't .... children under three. There are too many small pieces.

5 My sister graduated top of her class. The whole family is really .... her.

6 We should all be more .... each other. It's not difficult to say 'please' and 'thank you'.

7 I'm the manager. I'm .... the whole company, including 20 staff.

8 Teresa was .... an important meeting today. Her boss wasn't happy about that.

9 I'm .... my girlfriend. How could she forget my birthday?

10 I'm .... cooking. I burn everything!

11 We're all very .... your help. We couldn't have done it without you.

12 Where have you been? Your mother was really .... you! Why didn't you call to say you were all right?

verbs and prepositions

5 **Write the prepositions in the box in the correct place to complete the table.**

at	for	from	of	on	to

1	4
apologise apply ask look wait	belong invite lend listen reply
2 borrow choose prevent protect recover	**5** approve consist dream remind take care
3 concentrate decide depend plan insist	**6** laugh look point arrive stay

6 **Complete the sentences with a verb and preposition from Activity 5. You may need to change the form of the verb.**

1 I usually .... my little sister when my parents go out.

2 I've left my purse at home. Can I .... some money .... you?

3 It can take two or more weeks to .... flu.

4 Kirsty doesn't have a car so she .... her brother to take her to class.

5 My parents don't .... my boyfriend. They want me to break up with him.

6 Please be quiet! I'm trying to .... my work.

7 You .... me .... your father. You have the same smile.

8 Noel sent me an email this morning but I haven't .... him yet.

9 Where have you been? We've been .... you for two hours!

10 This isn't my book. Do you know who it .... ?

11 When I am in London, I like to .... my favourite hotel in the Strand.

12 The flight was delayed so it took over six hours for us to .... our destination.

verbs and noun phrases

7 Write the verbs in the box in the correct place to complete the table.

do   have   make   take

1	a photo a trip medicine a test/an exam	**3**	a coffee a shower fun a temperature
2	a mistake a noise money progress	**4**	homework the housework the washing-up your best

8 Complete the sentences with the verbs in the box. You may need to change the form of the verb.

break   do   gain   give   have   keep   make
pay   perform   print   run   save

1 When was the last time you .... a lot of fun?
2 Do you spend all your money or are you good at .... some of it?
3 Do you .... more noise than your neighbours or are they noisier than you?
4 Would you like to be an actor and .... on stage in front of hundreds of people?
5 Are you any good at .... a secret or do you tell everybody?
6 Would you like to .... your own business in the future?
7 Which world record would you like to ....?
8 Do you read documents on your computer screen or do you prefer to .... them and read them on paper?
9 Have you ever offered your time for free in order to .... work experience?
10 In what situations do you have to .... a deposit in your country?
11 Do you mind .... housework?
12 Do you .... your parents a call every day?

9 Answer the questions in Activity 8.

Word formation

prefixes

1 Write the prefixes in the box in the correct place to complete the table.

dis-   im-   ir-   un-

1	2	3	4 ....
mature patient perfect personal polite possible	regular replaceable responsible	acceptable avoidable fortunate pleasant reasonable reliable	loyal honest pleased respectful satisfied

2 Look at the underlined prefixes in sentences 1–4 and match them with questions A–D.

1 We won't all fit into one taxi. We need a <u>mini</u>bus.
2 David drove <u>non-</u>stop through the night to get here on time.
3 I forgot to save my report so I had to <u>re</u>type it.
4 William is very <u>self</u>-confident.

A Which prefix means *again*?
B Which prefix means *small*?
C Which prefix means *of, to, by* or *for yourself*?
D Which prefix means *not*?

3 Complete the words in the sentences with a prefix from Activities 1 and 2.

1 Are young people more ....respectful than the previous generation?
2 Do you get angry easily or do you have ....-control?
3 Have you ever had to ....do work on the computer because you forgot to save it?
4 Were you a mature or ....mature child?
5 Have you ever had a ....-break (a holiday for two or three nights)?
6 Do you prefer to read fiction or ....-fiction books?
7 Do you think it's a good idea to ....train when you're older and do something different?
8 Do you have a friend who's fun but ....reliable?

4 Answer the questions in Activity 3.

suffixes

5 Write the prefixes in the box in the correct place to complete the table.

-able   -ful   -less   -ment   -ly   -y

1 **noun +** .... → **adjective**	hair, fog, fun, noise, rain, sun
2 **adjective +** .... → **adverb**	annoying, calm, loud, patient, quiet, slow
3 **verb +** .... → **adjective meaning *can***	accept, achieve, change, love, move, pleasure
4 **noun +** .... → **adjective meaning *no***	care, colour, harm, hope, taste, use
5 **noun +** .... → **noun meaning *full of***	care, colour, harm, hope, taste, use
6 **verb +** .... → **noun**	advertise, announce, disagree, disappoint, employ, involve

6 Use the suffixes *-or* , *-er* and *-ist* to form job words for the words in the box.

act   art   build   design   direct   farm   instruct
journalism   photograph   report   sail   science

7 Add a suffix to the words in brackets to complete the sentences.

1 Do you think that it is ever .... (*accept*) to hit someone?
2 Have you ever had to drive or travel when it's really .... (*fog*)?
3 Are you creative enough to be a .... (*design*)?
4 Would you make a good .... (*act*)?
5 Has anyone ever complained that you're playing music too .... (*loud*)?
6 Have you ever had a big .... (*disagree*) with one of your close friends?
7 What was the last .... (*pleasure*) experience that you had?
8 Are you a good driver or are you .... (*care*)?
9 Do you wait in queues .... (*patient*) or do you get annoyed?
10 What has caused you .... (*disappoint*) or regret this year?

8 Answer the questions in Activity 7.

compound nouns

9 Match the first half of the sentences (1–8) with the second (A–H).

1 She's a model and has been on magazine
2 We need a new light
3 When a judge walks into the law
4 Would you like to come to a fitness
5 There's live
6 Drivers should stop at a pedestrian
7 People are worried that global
8 The staff at this hotel need to improve their customer

A court, everyone must stand up.
B covers around the world.
C crossing and let people cross the road.
D class with me?
E warming will cause many problems in future.
F bulb in the lamp in the bedroom.
G service if they want to keep their guests.
H entertainment at the hotel every evening.

10 Use one word from each box to form compound nouns and complete the sentences. Be careful with spelling: some compound nouns are written as one word.

exchange   hard   information   music
railway   show   sign   snow

business   disk   festival   line   pack   post
storm   visit

1 I'd love to have a job in .... I think I'd be a good TV presenter.
2 What's the name of this street? Can you see a .... anywhere?
3 Coldplay are playing at a big .... near my house next month.
4 I need to delete some of the files on my computer because the .... is full.
5 The train had to stop because there were cows on the ....
6 Some French students came to our college as part of an ....
7 Please collect an .... from reception. It contains a map and guide to the college.
8 It's freezing outside. A .... is coming.

compound adjectives

11 **Match the first half of the sentences (1–8) with the second (A–H).**

1 He's a good-
2 Both my parents have full-
3 We've just booked a last-
4 Using scissors is difficult for left-
5 The bag is expensive because it's hand-
6 I love my job. It's well-
7 Your children are polite and well-
8 Help yourself to food. This is a self-

A time jobs.
B minute trip to Paris. We're leaving tomorrow!
C service restaurant.
D behaved.
E paid and fun.
F looking man!
G made.
H handed people.

12 **Use one word from each box to form compound adjectives and complete the sentences.**

broken-	energy-	home-	long-	never-
one-	two-	world-		

distance	efficient	ending	famous
hearted	hour	made	way

1 Is this film going to finish soon? It seems to be ....!
2 When my girlfriend broke up with me, I was ....
3 We've got a special .... lesson tonight, from 6 to 8 p.m.
4 I'm not sure I can afford the bus fare. How much is a .... ticket to Hull?
5 My brother has never been on a .... flight before.
6 Enrique Iglesias is a .... singer.
7 There's .... lighting all around our house to help us save money.
8 Here, try one of Carla's .... biscuits. They're delicious!

Phrasal verbs

phrasal verbs with *up*

1 **Match the underlined phrasal verbs in sentences 1–8 with definitions A–H.**

1 She's decided to <u>give up</u> tennis after the tournament.
2 I'll arrive at the station at 10 p.m. Can you <u>pick</u> me <u>up</u>?
3 We couldn't find a restaurant that was open so we <u>ended up</u> getting a takeaway.
4 I can't believe she <u>hung up</u> without saying goodbye!
5 Andy was <u>brought up</u> by his aunt and uncle.
6 I'm sorry I'm late. I was <u>held up</u> by the traffic.
7 You're doing a really good job. <u>Keep up</u> the good work!
8 Do you have a dictionary? I need to <u>look</u> this word <u>up</u>.

A delay   E stop
B collect   F continue
C find information about   G end a phone call
D raise   H finally have to

2 **Complete the sentences with a phrasal verb from Activity 1. You may need to change the form of the verb.**

1 Can you .... the train times on that website?
2 I'm going to .... my job. I hate it!
3 I want to .... my children in a big family.
4 No! Don't ....! We need to talk!

phrasal verbs with *on*

3 **Match the underlined phrasal verbs in sentences 1–8 with definitions A–H.**

1 I've never <u>got on</u> with my brother. We argue all the time.
2 If you <u>carry on</u> ironing, I'll make dinner.
3 How do you <u>turn on</u> the washing machine?
4 You'll need to <u>put</u> your coat <u>on</u> when you go out. It's cold.
5 I must go and <u>get on with</u> making dinner.
6 <u>Come on</u>! We're going to be late!
7 If you <u>get on</u> the train first, I'll pass your bags to you.
8 The family down the road <u>keeps on</u> having loud parties.

A make something work   E put clothes on your body
B continue   F hurry
C enter (transport)   G have a friendly relationship
D do something many times   H make progress with

4 **Complete the sentences with a phrasal verb from Activity 3. You may need to change the form of the verb.**

1   We .... with our neighbours really well. They often come round for dinner.
2   Stop talking and .... your work!
3   My little sister .... taking my clothes without asking!
4   When her friend left, she .... working on her project.

phrasal verbs with *off*

5 **Match the underlined phrasal verbs in sentences 1–8 with definitions A–H.**

1   We got up early so we could <u>set off</u> before the traffic got bad.
2   The plane <u>took off</u> at 5 a.m.
3   Don't forget to <u>switch off</u> the TV before you go to bed.
4   Kerry <u>got off</u> the bus at the wrong stop and had to walk for a mile!
5   Ewan's sick so we have to <u>put</u> the meeting <u>off</u> until next Friday.
6   Why have the lights <u>gone off</u>?
7   I had a terrible headache this morning but the pain's <u>worn off</u> now.
8   It's really hot in here. Why don't you <u>take off</u> your coat?

A   exit (transport)
B   stop working
C   stop (something) working
D   change to a later date
E   remove (clothes from your body)
F   start a journey
G   move off the ground into the air
H   disappear (feeling/effect)

6 **Complete the sentences with a phrasal verb from Activity 5. You may need to change the form of the verb.**

1   Is the TV broken? It just .... for no reason.
2   I felt great this morning but that feeling has .... Now I just feel tired!
3   I .... for work at 7.30 a.m. every morning.
4   The hall is booked next week so I've .... the party .... until the week after.

phrasal verbs with *out*

7 **Match the underlined phrasal verbs in sentences 1–8 with definitions A–H.**

1   Sarah, please <u>hand out</u> a worksheet to everyone.
2   I want a hot drink but we've <u>run out of</u> coffee.
3   At the weekends I <u>hang out</u> with my friends.
4   We <u>set out</u> for the woods just after sunrise.
5   Jack is <u>going out</u> with Melissa.
6   We've got a problem that we need to <u>sort out</u>.
7   Can you <u>find out</u> who that woman is?
8   I thought I'd emailed everyone but I'd <u>left</u> Kevin <u>out</u>.

A   start a journey
B   not include
C   give something to each person in a group
D   spend time
E   organise or solve
F   use all of something so there's no more left
G   get information about
H   date

8 **Complete the sentences with a phrasal verb from Activity 7. You may need to change the form of the verb.**

1   Do you know how long Sun and Jin have been .... together?
2   Stu .... on his trip with a backpack and a tent.
3   We all sat down and the teacher .... the exam papers.
4   I got paid last week but I've .... money already!

phrasal verbs with other particles

9 **Match the underlined phrasal verbs in sentences 1–8 with definitions A–H.**

1   Our car has <u>broken down</u> again!
2   Who is <u>looking after</u> your cat while you're away?
3   I <u>threw away</u> those old magazines.
4   I sometimes <u>call in on</u> my grandparents on the way home from college.
5   That shirt I bought was too small so I <u>took</u> it <u>back</u>.
6   I'm absolutely exhausted! I'm really <u>looking forward to</u> the weekend.
7   Does this shirt <u>go with</u> these trousers?
8   We <u>checked in</u> at the hotel at noon.

A visit someone while going somewhere else

B stop working

C return

D be excited about something that's going to happen

E match

F put something in a bin

G go to the desk to say you have arrived

H take care of

10 **Complete the sentences with a phrasal verb from Activity 9. You may need to change the form of the verb.**

1 Don't worry about me. I can .... myself!

2 We're all .... seeing Mark again – we haven't seen him since high school.

3 I'll .... you on my way home and give you the money I owe you.

4 What's this rubbish doing here? Why haven't you .... it ....?

Different meanings of *get*

1 **Match the verbs in the box with the different meanings of *get* in the sentences.**

arrive	become	buy	find	receive	improve
move	prepare				

1 When you go to the supermarket, could you <u>get</u> me a loaf of bread, please?

2 On my birthday, I <u>got</u> a book from my mother.

3 My sore throat isn't <u>getting better</u> – I may have to go to the doctor.

4 I'll call you when I <u>get</u> to the airport.

5 <u>Get</u> away from the edge of the pool – you'll fall in!

6 My friend's trying to <u>get</u> a new job – she really hates working in an office.

7 I'm going to put my coat on – I'm <u>getting</u> cold.

8 My sister takes ages to <u>get ready</u> to go out!

Easily confused words

1 **Choose the correct alternative in each sentence.**

1 May I have a glass of orange juice, please, and a *package / packet* of crisps?

2 I don't believe she'd do something so stupid – she's usually very *sensible / sensitive*.

3 A lot of *strangers / foreigners* visit London every year from all over the world.

4 I often ask for *advice / advise* from my big sister.

5 He *told / said* me all about his weekend at the beach.

6 In my *opinion / idea*, people should take more exercise!

7 If you visit Scotland, you'll see some wonderful *nature / scenery*.

8 Please *remind / remember* me to send my brother a birthday card!

9 Can you *borrow / lend* me some money until tomorrow? I've left my purse at home.

10 Dont' forget to *bring / take* me back a souvenir from your holiday!

Same sound, different spelling

1 **Choose the correct alternative in each sentence.**

1 I love all sport *accept / except* football.

2 I love going to Italy – the food is so good *their / there*.

3 I'm sorry – I didn't *here / hear* what you said.

4 I hope the *weather / whether* is good on Saturday for our picnic.

5 I can't *see / sea* the screen very well – can we change our seats?

6 *Where / Wear* did you meet your friend?

Common errors: Preliminary

1 Find and correct the mistakes with questions.

1 What your name?
2 Where you from?
3 What you do?
4 Where you going?
5 How many times you been outside your country?
6 What you enjoy most about the experience?

2 Find and correct the mistakes with indirect questions.

1 Would you mind telling me how do I get to the station from here?
2 Can you tell me when was the microscope invented?
3 I'd like to know if you did enjoy the party.
4 Could you tell me what do you find easiest about learning English?
5 I'd like to know whether am I allowed to have friends come to stay.
6 Would you mind telling me how do you spell your surname?

3 Find and correct the mistakes with the present simple and present continuous.

1 People who lives in glass houses shouldn't throw stones.
2 My sister ride her bicycle to college every day.
3 When do you coming to visit us again?
4 I going away for the weekend so I'll be a bit late on Monday.
5 My brother don't like hip hop music.
6 You takes the tram to La Laguna. It stop opposite the university.

4 Find and correct the mistakes with modals of possibility.

1 He must to be exhausted. The match has been going on for over five hours.
2 It mustn't be the postman. He never comes this early.
3 I'll answer the phone if you like. It can be for me.
4 We can to meet on Wednesday or Thursday. I don't mind.
5 Take an umbrella, just in case. It must rain later.
6 When I finish college, I might to go and work in another country.

5 Find and correct the mistakes with -*ing* forms and infinitives.

1 If you ask me, to buy a new computer is a waste of money.
2 She apologised for arrive late.
3 I'm better at watch tennis than I am at play it.
4 Would you mind to pass the salt?
5 We're looking forward to hear about your holiday in Greece.
6 We've arranged meeting outside the cinema at 5.30.

6 Find and correct the mistakes with modals of obligation.

1 You must not to walk on the grass.
2 I has to go. See you later.
3 Have we to buy a book or is the teacher going to give us photocopies?
4 If you want to lose weight, you don't have to eat so many cakes and sweets.
5 Do I should wear a hat to the wedding?
6 Sue won't be here next Tuesday. She must go to the dentist.

7 Find and correct the mistakes with the present perfect, past simple and *used to*.

Simon: (1) Did you ever go to Paris?

Clare: (2) Yes, several times. In fact, I have gone last November.

Simon: (3) A friend of mine has been last year. He says it's very expensive.

Clare: (4) Well, it used to be but this time I have found it quite cheap.

Simon: (5) Where have you stayed?

Clare: (6) In a little hotel near the Sorbonne. It was there for ages. My great-grandfather has stayed there every time he has gone to Paris.

8 Find and correct the mistakes with *so, such, too* and *enough*.

1 We had a so good time at the party.
2 Susan is such nice person.
3 This tiramisu is such delicious! Can I have some more?
4 You're not enough old to stay out after midnight.
5 Snowboarding is so fun. I love it.
6 I'm afraid the exam was too much difficult for me. I don't think I'll pass.

9 Find and correct the mistakes with comparatives and superlatives in the candidate's answers below.

1 Tina is better at salsa dancing than me.
  I am not ＿＿good at＿＿ salsa dancing as Tina.
2 My sense of rhythm is worse than Tina's.
  Tina has ＿＿a good＿＿ sense of rhythm than me.
3 There is no one in the salsa class that is as bad as Carey.
  Carey is ＿＿worst＿＿ in the salsa class.
4 Carey can't even dance as well as Ivan.
  Carey is even ＿more bad than＿ Ivan.

10 Find and correct the mistakes with the past simple.

1 Where does your father live when he was a child?
2 Who winned the Eurovision song contest last year?
3 We all feeled ill after the meal.
4 I fell in love with Fernando the first time I seed him.
5 We buyed Mum some perfume for her birthday.
6 I catched a terrible cold while I was in London.

11 Find and correct the mistakes with the past simple and past continuous.

1 Alex listened to some music on his phone while the teacher was telling us what to do for homework.
2 Some of the contestants were rehearsing when the stage was collapsing.
3 I was phoning my friend on her mobile when I was seeing her standing on the corner.
4 You were sitting there watching the match while I cooked the dinner!
5 I had a shower when the telephone rang.
6 Tim slept soundly while the burglars were stealing his new flat-screen TV.

12 Find and correct the mistakes with the past perfect.

1 As soon as I had got to school, I remembered that the teacher had told us there was going to be an exam that day.
2 I felt really nervous because I missed lots of lectures.
3 By the time I got to the classroom, the teacher already started the exam.
4 I had hardly looked at the questions when I had seen that the boy sitting next to me had written almost a whole page.
5 When the teacher had told us to stop writing, I had only answered two of the three questions.
6 I was sure I failed but, in fact, in the end I got quite a good mark.

13 Find and correct the mistakes with countable and uncountable nouns.

1 She was wearing a trousers and a jacket.
2 Are we having a chicken for dinner again?
3 She's got a lovely dark curly hair.
4 How many money do you spend on food and entertainment each week?
5 There are too many furnitures in this room.

14 Find and correct the mistakes with articles.

1 I love living here because sun shines almost every day.
2 There's volcano here that is almost 4,000 metres high.
3 I prefer living on coast to living in countryside though.
4 It's wonderful to be able to swim in sea every day.
5 There's also lake near here which has very clear water.
6 I sometimes go there at night and swim in the light of moon.

15 Find and correct the mistakes with reported speech.

1 She said me that she would be a little bit late.
2 I told to the neighbours that I was going to be away for a few days.
3 Tim told that he would be home on Saturday night.
4 Tanya said that she can't ride a bicycle.
5 Paulo told me he is coming on Monday.
6 Gustave said he will be here by midday but he still hasn't arrived.

16 Find and correct the mistakes with reported questions.

1 She asked me how was I feeling.
2 She asked us did we enjoy our English course.
3 She asked me have I any special plans for the future.
4 She asked me what are you going to do when you finish university.
5 She asked me is there anything special I want to do in the future.
6 She asked me what kinds of things did I like doing in my spare time.

17 Find and correct the mistakes with modals of ability.

1 I can understand the news on the radio now but I can't even understand my teacher a few months ago.
2 I could read short books in English now but I couldn't even read a newspaper at the beginning of the course.
3 I was able to write stories, reports and articles in English now but I can't even write an informal letter when we started using this book.
4 I can express my opinion in English now but I cannot even talk about a photo properly last September.
5 I could pronounce most words quite well now but I can't even understand the pronunciation symbols in the dictionary at the beginning of the course.

18 Find and correct the mistakes with relative clauses.

1 Tina, that came to your party, is living in Paris now.
2 Thor Heyerdahl that died in 2000 discovered some pyramids on the island of Tenerife.
3 She's the girl I told you about her.
4 Tim's the boy who's father is a politician.
5 Is Fabio the boy which is going to France next year?

19 Find and correct the mistakes with future forms.

1 Oh no! I think I'm being sick.
2 I have to go now. I phone you back later.
3 What do you do next year when you finish school?
4 What time your plane leave?
5 Look at those dark clouds! It rains later.
6 I've already decided. I'll buy Ella a CD for her birthday.

20 Find and correct the mistakes with conditionals.

1 How would you feel if you don't get enough sleep?
2 What would you say if you meet someone famous?
3 Who do you usually talk to when you were worried about something?
4 How do you feel if Australia won the World Cup?
5 What do you do this summer if you can't afford to go on holiday?
6 What would you buy if you would have £100,000?

21 Look at these extracts from candidates' answers and the teacher's comments. Find and correct the mistakes with vocabulary and spelling.

1 My boyfriend is quite well-build. He's medium-hieght (about 1.80) and a little bit overwieght but I still think he's very hansome. The thing I like most about him though is that he is always very honnest.

Watch your spelling.

2 You'll love our house in the mountains. In the winter, when it's been snowing outside, we all sit around the chimney and talk after dinner. It's so cosy. It can be quite hot in summer but, luckily, we have air-conditioned so we keep nice and cool. I hope you can come next year.

You've used the wrong word in one sentence and the wrong word form in another.

3 The person in my family I get through with best is my older sister. We're really good friends. She's about seven years older than me so she looked for me and my younger brother a lot when we were little.

Check your phrasal verbs.

4 I couldn't work up the meaning of a word and I decided to look up it in a dictionary. It wasn't there so I looked in it online but I couldn't find it there either. In the end I gave out and decided to ask the teacher.

Check your phrasal verbs.

5 A lot of people criticise it but I get a lot of enjoy from watching television. I even like the advertisings.

Be careful with word forms.

6 I wanted to buy a new top because at the hot weather. There were some nice ones in sale on a shop near here. I tried one out but I wasn't very keen for the way it looked at me. I'm really tired with looking at clothes that fit me. I never find anything!

Check your prepositions.

89

Exam strategies

In the exam you need to think of strategies that will help you to do the exam tasks. Here are some tips for each paper and examples of mistakes students often make.

Reading and Writing (Paper 1)

General advice: Reading and Writing

- Read different things in English as there are different types of text in Paper 1.
- Don't look up every word in a dictionary. Try to work out the meaning of the word first.
- When you are writing, make a list of things to check when you have finished (e.g. spelling and grammar).
- Always check that your writing is relevant to the task.
- Practise writing things in different ways as this will help make your writing more interesting.

General exam tips: Reading

- Read all the instructions carefully. They tell you something about what you will read.
- The answers are always there in the texts, even if you don't see them at first.
- Don't worry if you don't understand a word – you may be able to guess its meaning.

Reading Part 1: Three-option multiple choice

1 Match the advice (1–3) with the explanations (A–C).

1 Think about what the person who reads or sees the message has to do.

2 Be careful if you see the same word in the text and in the option.

3 Think about the purpose or reason for the message.

A This does not mean it is the answer – you should look for synonyms.

B This tells you what the message or sign really means, not just the words.

C The meaning of the message or sign may tell you to do something.

2 In the question below, a candidate chose option B. Which piece of advice from Activity 1 did the candidate forget? What is the correct answer?

> *Don't turn this computer off – I'm still working on it. I'll be back in ten minutes. Please go to the computer in the library if you need one immediately.*
>
> **A** Wait ten minutes before using this computer.
> **B** The computer must be turned off after ten minutes.
> **C** There is another computer that can be used.

Reading Part 2: Matching

3 **Match 1–3 with A–C to complete the advice.**

1 Highlight what each person needs

2 Choose the option that matches everything the person needs

3 Check your answers

A as some may only match some of their needs.

B because it makes it easier for you to see matches.

C so you don't choose an option more than once.

4 **In the question below about films to rent, a candidate chose this option, which is wrong. Which piece of advice from Activity 3 did the candidate forget?**

> Sue wants to rent a film to watch. She likes true stories but prefers them to have a happy ending. She doesn't like musicals.
>
> *This film is about a real-life dancer who fights her way to the top in very difficult circumstances. The final scenes are heart-warming and the songs add emotion and fun. An enjoyable film!*

Reading Part 3: True/False

5 **Complete the advice.**

1 The words in the questions will not be the same as in the text. Look for s............................ of words in the statement, not identical words.

2 A true statement must have the same general meaning as the words in the text. Check that the statement means e............................ the same as the text.

3 The information in the text is given in the same order as the questions. Don't look for information in d............................ parts of the text.

6 **Read the extract from a text and the statement below. A candidate said that the statement is true. Why was the candidate's answer wrong?**

> The tour will stop for an afternoon in the small medieval town, where you will wander round the market, spend time in the museum and then climb the hill above the town to admire the view. Alternatively, you can relax by sitting in the beautiful gardens and enjoying the flowers.
>
> *The afternoon will be full of activities, with no chance to rest.*

Reading Part 4: Four-option multiple choice

7 **Complete the advice with the words and phrases in the box.**

before   opinions and feelings   writer's purpose

1 The first question is about the .... so you should think about the meaning of function words like *comparing*, *arguing*, *suggesting* and *explaining*.

2 Many questions ask about .... so you should also look for these in the text, not just detailed information.

3 Only one option is correct so you should check that the others are wrong .... making your final decision.

8 **Which pieces of advice from Activity 7 do you need to follow for this question?**

> What is the writer doing in this text?
>
> A giving information about people who are celebrities
>
> B suggesting why being a celebrity is not always enjoyable
>
> C explaining why he wants to be a celebrity
>
> D giving advice on how to become a celebrity

Reading Part 5: Four-option multiple-choice cloze

9 **Read the statements about Reading Part 5 and decide if they are true or false.**

1 Not all the questions test vocabulary. Grammar is tested too.

2 Some examples of things tested include phrasal verbs and fixed phrases.

3 The four options may have similar meanings but only one is correct in the text.

10 **What is the correct answer? Answer the questions, then match them with the advice in Activity 9.**

> 1 I really want to take .... golf – I've never had the chance to try it before.
>
>   A in   B at   C out   D up
>
> 2 I stopped running marathons because the long distance was .... difficult for me.
>
>   A far   B too   C such   D much
>
> 3 Jack wanted to .... playing tennis even though he wasn't very good.
>
>   A stay   B maintain   C remain   D continue

General exam tips: Writing

- Try to use a range of vocabulary and expressions, as well as different grammatical structures.
- Leave yourself enough time to check your writing for mistakes in spelling and grammar.
- In Part 3, read the two questions before choosing which one to answer. Make sure you have enough to say.

Writing Part 1: Sentence transformations

11 **Choose the correct alternative to complete the advice.**

A Make sure your sentence is *as close as possible / quite similar* to the original.

B Write *no more than / fewer than* three words.

C You *should try to / must* spell the words correctly.

12 **Look at a candidate's answers below, which are all incorrect. Which piece of advice from Activity 11 has the candidate forgotten in each sentence?**

1 She finished her meal before I got home.
  When I got home, she _had alreddy finished_ her meal.

2 I couldn't swim until I was 12.
  I was _____ able to _____ swim until I was 12.

3 Why don't you join a gym?
  If I were you, ___I would try to___ join a gym.

Writing Part 2: Short communicative message

13 **Find and correct the mistakes in the advice about Writing Part 2.**

1 You don't have to write about all three points in the task.

2 You should write more than 45 words.

3 You can write fewer than 35 words.

14 **Look at the exam task and the answer a candidate has written. Which two pieces of advice from Activity 13 has the candidate forgotten?**

> An English friend called Clara has sent you an unexpected present.
>
> Write an email to Clara. In your email you should:
> - thank her for the present.
> - explain how you felt about the present.
> - tell her you will send her something in return.
>
> Write 35–45 words.

Hi Clara,

I was so surprised to get the book you sent me but I love it! It was very kind of you to send it to me and I am very happy about it. It is a book I haven't read before and I think it is very interesting. I will read it on my holiday next month.

Thanks again!

Love,

Jo

Writing Part 3: Longer piece of continuous writing

15 **Look at the advice below and decide if each piece of advice is for the letter (L), the story (S) or both (B).**

In your extended writing, you should check that:

1 you have written about the right topic.

2 there are no spelling and grammar mistakes.

3 you have used a range of vocabulary and grammar.

4 you have written the right number of words.

5 you have used the correct opening and ending.

6 you have used language like adjectives to interest the reader.

16 Look at the exam task and the answer a candidate has written. Which three pieces of advice from Activity 15 has the candidate forgotten?

> Your English teacher has asked you to write a story.
> This is the title for your story:
> *An enjoyable day*
> Write your story in about 100 words.

> I was feeling sad because it was the weekend
> and all my freinds were busy. I wanted to
> go shopping but there was no one for me to
> go with. I was sitting at home reeding, when,
> sudenly, the phone rang. It was a girl from
> my old school who had moved to another
> town. She was visiting her old scool freinds
> and wanted to meet me to talk. We met in
> the local café and talked about everything we
> were doing. It was great to talk to her and so
> I had a very enjoyable day after al.

Listening (Paper 2)

General advice

- Listen to as many things in English as you can – use the radio and the internet.
- Don't worry if you don't hear or understand a word – relax and listen for the general meaning.

General exam tips

- Use the time you have to read through all the questions or look at the pictures.
- Read the instructions as you listen to them.
- Don't worry if you haven't chosen all the answers after the first listening.
- Use the second listening to get the answers you missed and to check your answers.
- Check that you have written your answers correctly on the answer sheet.

Listening Part 1: Multiple choice (discrete)

1 Match the advice (1–3) with the explanations (A–C).

1 Listen for key words in the question.
2 Listen for words like *best* or *most* in the question.
3 Don't worry about what you have to listen to.

A You may have to listen for something that someone likes best or most.
B You may hear conversations or monologues (one person speaking).
C You may hear vocabulary from all the pictures but only one picture will answer the question.

Listening Part 2: Multiple choice

2 Match 1–3 with A–C to complete the advice.

1 Listen carefully
2 Listen for tenses and connectors
3 Read the question carefully

A to check that the answer you choose really answers it.
B because the correct answer may not be the first one you hear.
C because the question may ask what happened first.

Listening Part 3: Gap-fill

3 Read the advice. Which explanation (A–D) is not correct?

Before you listen, you should read the question carefully because

A it helps to think about the kind of information to write in each space.
B you should check your spelling.
C you may hear numbers or times, and you should be prepared for this.
D you shouldn't write words that are already in the question.

Listening Part 4: True/False

4 **Complete the advice.**

1   Most of the questions focus on what the speakers think or feel. Look for and identify words in the question connected with the speakers' o............................... or a.................................. .

2   There may be a question about whether the speakers agree with each other. Wait until the speakers have finished their turns to see if the second speaker a................................ or not.

3   What the speakers say is in the same order as the questions. Don't listen for information in d.............................. parts of the conversation.

Speaking (Paper 3)

General advice

• Practise your English with friends whenever you can.
• Listen to English on the radio or the internet – it will help your confidence with speaking.
• Practise your pronunciation of new words with friends.

General exam tips

• Listen carefully to the examiner's instructions. Ask the examiner to repeat them if you are not sure what to do.
• Speak clearly so that the examiner can hear you.
• Don't worry if you make mistakes, and try not to feel nervous.

Speaking Part 1: Personal questions

1   Give interesting answers to the examiner's questions.
2   Don't prepare long speeches in advance.
3   Give natural answers and don't hesitate too much.
4   Don't worry about making mistakes.

1 **Look at the examiner's question and a candidate's answer below. Which two pieces of advice has the candidate forgotten?**

Q: What did you do last Saturday?

A: Last Saturday? Do you mean … er … that's a very good question. Er … I go … no, I went, yes, went to the cinema. Or did I went … er … go … to shopping? Er … I think …

Speaking Part 2: Simulated situation

1   Discuss all the pictures with your partner.
2   Say what you think and give reasons for your ideas.
3   Always ask your partner for their opinions and ideas.
4   Don't worry if you disagree with your partner.

2 **Look at this extract from a conversation between two candidates. Which piece of advice have they forgotten?**

A: Let's start with this. I think it's a good idea to buy flowers. Because she likes flowers. And I don't think it's a good idea to buy a book. She doesn't like reading.

B: I think it's a good idea to buy a pen because she writes a lot of letters.

A: I like the camera too but it's expensive.

Speaking Part 3: Extended turn

1   Try to describe everything you can see in your picture.
2   Don't worry if you don't know a word – just move on. You will not lose marks if you don't know a word.
3   The examiner will stop you after about a minute.

3 **Look at this extract from a long turn. Which piece of advice has the candidate forgotten?**

In the top corner I can see a … a … I don't know. It's a … maybe it's a … something like a box. I'm not sure.

Speaking Part 4: General conversation

1   Have a normal conversation with your partner about the topic the examiner gives you.
2   You should say what you think but you should also ask your partner what they think.
3   Try to give interesting details about your ideas.

4 **Look at this extract from a conversation between two candidates. Which two pieces of advice have they forgotten?**

I'd like you to talk about things you like to do in the evening, and things you don't like to do.

A: I like watching TV.

B: I like playing computer games.

A: I don't like reading books.

B: I don't like cooking.

Reading

Part I

Questions 1–5

Look at the text in each question.
What does it say?
Mark the correct letter, **A**, **B** or **C**, on your answer sheet.

Example:

0

The lift to the meeting room is out of order. Please use the stairs near the reception desk.

A You should go to the meeting room by using the stairs.

B You must use the stairs to reach reception.

C You can use the lift near reception to get to the meeting room.

Answer:

1

All books borrowed from the library must be returned before the end of July.

A You cannot borrow books until 31 July.

B If you have borrowed a book from the library, you have to take it back by 31 July.

C You can keep a book you have borrowed if you tell the library by 31 July.

2

NEXT WEEK'S COACH TRIP
There aren't any seats left on the coach. Anyone who asked to come on the trip and hasn't given me the money should do so before tomorrow.

A You have to pay for a reserved seat on the coach today.

B You can reserve a seat on the coach if you pay today.

C If you haven't paid for the trip yet, your seat on the coach will be given to someone else.

3

THESE TABLES ARE ONLY FOR CUSTOMERS EATING CAFÉ MEALS. PLEASE EAT YOUR OWN FOOD AT THE PICNIC TABLES OUTSIDE.

A You cannot eat food bought in the café at the picnic tables.

B If you want to eat at the tables, you have to bring your own food.

C You can eat at the café tables if you bought your food there.

4

From: Paloma
To: Erik

I think I left a book in your office. It was a present for Andrew and it's his birthday tomorrow!

What does Paloma want Erik to do?

A buy a present for Andrew

B give Andrew a book

C look for a book she bought

5

After opening keep refrigerated and use within 3–4 days.

A You can use this product four days after opening it.

B There is enough of this product for three to four days.

C You should not use this product after three to four days.

Part 2

Questions 6–10

The people below are all looking for a fitness course.
On page 98 there are eight advertisements.
Decide which course would be the most suitable for the following people.
For questions **6–10**, mark the correct letter **(A–H)** on your answer sheet.

---

6 Yolanda would like to do gentle exercise in the open air in the evenings. She likes to do things with groups of older people.

7 Bashir likes meeting people, team sports and competition. He wants to improve his sporting skills and get stronger and fitter. He is free two afternoons a week.

8 Vikash doesn't have much free time. He wants to be able to exercise for an hour a day in the evenings or early morning. He prefers to do things on his own.

9 Laurent wants something he can do with his wife and teenage children. They all enjoy being outdoors, especially at the seaside. He only has weekends free.

10 Tomoko is very interested in other cultures. She would like to learn to do something that is good exercise but not too tiring. She finishes work at 4.30 p.m.

Fitness courses

A **Sarasvati Yoga School**
In our large mixed ability classes, you can work at your own relaxed speed and learn about yoga in ancient India. From 7 to 9 a.m. and 6 to 8 p.m., on Mondays and Fridays.

B **Running training**
Join us for running training every Tuesday and Thursday in Anderson Park. The complete run starts at 5 p.m. and takes an hour. Fit adults only.

C **Fitness Fans' Gym**
We're open every day from 7 a.m. to midnight. Personal fitness trainers will study your individual needs and design an exercise programme just for you.

D **Sports Club**
Do you want to make new friends, train with others, get professional coaching and play in matches? Get fit and develop your abilities! Join the Sports Club!

E **Water aerobics**
Have fun and get fit in the Wilson indoor pool. Much easier than normal aerobics and great for teenagers. Classes every afternoon from four to five.

F **Beach volleyball**
Join us every Sunday morning at Sunnysands beach. Kids and adults are welcome to take part. We're not professionals. We just play for fun and exercise!

G **Tara's T'ai Chi**
Most of our members are people in their forties, fifties and sixties who enjoy the gentle movements of T'ai Chi. All our classes are held in Anderson Park. Week nights from 6 to 8 p.m.

H **Ballroom dancing**
Dance your way to fitness in our ballroom dancing class. Perfect for couples. You'll sleep well after two hours of movement! Evenings from 9.30.

Part 3

Questions 11–20

Look at the sentences below about Cornwall in the west of England.
Read the text on page 100 to decide if each sentence is correct or incorrect.
If it is correct, mark **A** on your answer sheet.
If it is not correct, mark **B** on your answer sheet.

---

11 No other part of the English mainland is further west than Lands End.

12 There is only one lighthouse near Lands End.

13 People often see sharks near the Scilly Isles.

14 A lot of artists and writers live in St Ives.

15 Every time you surf at Fistral you can expect to see the Cribbar.

16 The traditional parade in Padstow takes place once a year.

17 You can't take a boat from Padstow harbour to the islands in the winter.

18 Some people were not sure about the connection between King Arthur and Tintagel.

19 Cornish pasties are made all over Britain.

20 You need a knife and fork to eat a pasty.

Cornwall

Cornwall is the UK's most popular holiday destination and with all it has to offer, this is not surprising. So how can you make the most of your Cornish holiday?

A good place to begin is Lands End, the most westerly point in mainland England. There are spectacular cliffs over 300 feet high and you can see the famous Longships Lighthouse about a mile out to sea. This lighthouse, which is one of several in the area, warns ships of the dangerous rocks along the coast here. On a clear day the nearby Scilly Isles can be seen and you might notice some dolphins or even a shark, though they are quite rare.

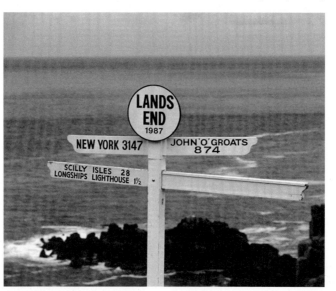

If what you are looking for is a beach holiday, then you really must spend some time in St Ives. There are actually several beaches here, all with fine golden sand and clean water. The town itself is charming and has a resident population of artists and writers.

Surfers will want to head for Fistral Beach near Newquay, probably the best surfing beach in Cornwall. Fistral is in a perfect position for the big waves the Atlantic Ocean can produce. When the conditions are right, a really enormous wave called the Cribbar comes in. Expert surfers only, please!

Padstow is the place to go for a taste of real Cornish traditions. Every year locals and tourists fill the streets of this pretty village for the famous May Day parade. In the spring and summer months you can take a boat trip from the harbour and stop on one of the many tiny islands or just enjoy the views of the spectacular coastline.

Historians will put Tintagel at the top of their list of places to visit. People have been living here since Iron Age times but it is the link to King Arthur and Camelot that attracts so many tourists in the summer months. There has been doubt about this link in the past but the recent discovery of the Arthnou Stone, with some words dating from about the sixth century, seems to prove that King Arthur really did live here.

There's plenty more to see and do but before you leave for home, make sure you try Cornwall's national dish, the pasty. And it is now official: Cornish pasties must be made in Cornwall, although the ingredients, beef, onion, potato and turnip, can come from other parts of the UK. All the ingredients are packed into a case made of flour and water called pastry, and baked in the oven and they can be eaten in the hands. Perfect for a picnic! You can get them everywhere but if you are lucky enough to be in the village of Polruan on the day of the annual regatta, you will see a giant pasty paraded through the streets.

Part 4

Questions 21–25

Read the text and questions on page 102.
For each question, mark the correct letter, **A**, **B**, **C** or **D** on your answer sheet.

My Homeshare experience

I looked for a flat when I first came to London but it was really very difficult. I didn't like the idea of sharing with other students. I've seen a lot of student flats and they are sometimes dirty and often untidy. Living on my own wasn't possible because it was just too expensive.

That's when I discovered the Homeshare service. Elderly people who need help around the house offer to share their home with a younger person who needs accommodation. Instead of paying rent, the younger person agrees to help with jobs around the house. These are usually light cleaning and cooking but the most important thing you do is talk to the elderly person for a while. They're often very lonely.

Marjorie was. She's 74 and her husband died 20 years ago. She's a fantastic storyteller and a very clever person. I like to cook and we eat together at least four times a week. That gives us a chance to be together and talk. Marjorie asks me to do quite a lot of cleaning but that's not a problem for me. Homeshare has been great for both of us. It's given me somewhere to stay and both of us a new friend.

21 What is the writer's main purpose in writing the text?

A to describe her everyday life

B to talk about a flat she has lived in

C to explain a service she thinks is very good

D to say why it was difficult to find a flat

22 What would a reader learn about the writer from reading the text?

A She likes her home to be clean and tidy.

B She prefers to live alone.

C She knew about Homeshare before she came to London.

D She can afford to live by herself.

23 How does the writer think she helps Marjorie most?

A by spending time with her

B by doing the cleaning

C by cooking her meals

D by paying for her accommodation

24 How does the writer feel about Marjorie?

A She feels sorry for her.

B She admires her.

C She thinks she too demanding.

D She is worried about her.

25 Which of the following best describes the writer?

A a young person who couldn't find any other young people to share a flat with

B a young person who enjoys sharing her home with an older person

C a young person who has to work in another person's house

D a young person who would prefer to live alone

Part 5

Questions 26–35

Read the text below and choose the correct word for each space.
For each question, mark the correct letter, **A**, **B**, **C** or **D**, on your answer sheet.

Example:

0   **A** also   **B** and   **C** too   **D** plus

Answer:

A jungle painting

A school ran some art classes in the evenings. The classes were not only for school students but **(0)** .... for people from the town, and were very successful – **(26)** .... of people came to learn how to become artists. The most popular classes were on **(27)** .... to draw and paint animals.

The school buildings had been **(28)** .... a long time ago and were quite dark and not very beautiful. The people on the art course wanted to add **(29)** .... colour to the school and to **(30)** .... something that would stay there for a long time. **(31)** .... they decided to paint a huge picture on the front wall, showing a jungle scene with lots of different animals hiding **(32)** .... the trees. Everyone enjoyed working together on the project, **(33)** .... took ten weeks to finish. The school students now feel very happy with their colourful school and the art students are very **(34)** .... of their work. Who knows what the art class students are **(35)** .... of painting next?

---

26 **A** lots   **B** many   **C** much   **D** few

27 **A** what   **B** why   **C** how   **D** where

28 **A** produced   **B** developed   **C** grown   **D** built

29 **A** any   **B** some   **C** bit   **D** little

30 **A** create   **B** bring   **C** put   **D** give

31 **A** Because   **B** So   **C** As   **D** But

32 **A** among   **B** with   **C** up   **D** through

33 **A** that   **B** who   **C** which   **D** when

34 **A** pleased   **B** happy   **C** glad   **D** proud

35 **A** planning   **B** deciding   **C** thinking   **D** hoping

Writing

Part 1

Questions 1–5

Here are some sentences about a family staying in a hotel by the sea.
For each question, complete the second sentence so that it means the same as the first.
Use no more than three words.
Write only the missing words on your answer sheet.
You may use this page for any rough work.

Example:

0   It took us a long time to choose our hotel.

We took a long time .... **our hotel.**

Answer: | **0** | *choosing* |

---

1   It was several years since we had stayed in a hotel by the sea.

We had not stayed in a hotel by the sea .... **several years.**

2   The rooms were very surprising because they were so big.

We were very .... **the rooms because they were so big.**

3   The food in the restaurant was great, though the service was not so good.

The food in the restaurant was .... **the service.**

4   There was a large swimming pool in the hotel garden.

The hotel garden .... **a large swimming pool.**

5   But we were unlucky because there was rain every day!

But we were unlucky because it .... **every day!**

Part 2

Question 6

You have just spent a day out with a friend, Emily, and her family at an adventure park.
Write a card to Emily. In your card you should:

* thank Emily for the day.

* say what you enjoyed most about the day.

* ask Emily to spend a day with you next week.

Write **35–45 words** on your answer sheet.

Part 3

Write an answer to one of the questions (**7** or **8**) in this part.
Write your answer in about **100 words** on your answer sheet.
Tick the box (Question 7 or Question 8) on your answer sheet to show which question you have answered.

Question 7

* This is part of a letter you receive from your English friend John.

> I have to write about a special holiday people have in your
> country for my college magazine. What do you think I should
> write about? What do people do on the day?

* Now write a letter to John.

* Write your **letter** in about 100 words on your answer sheet.

Question 8

* Your English teacher has asked you to write a story.

* This is the title for your story:
  The most enjoyable day of my life

* Write your **story** in about 100 words on your answer sheet.

Paper 2   Listening

Part 1 ▶44

Questions 1–7

There are seven questions in this part.

For each question, there are three pictures and a short recording.
Choose the correct picture and put a tick (✓) in the box below it.

Example: Where are the woman's car keys?

A ☐   B ☐   C ☑

---

1   What time does the film start?

A ☐   B ☐   C ☐

2   What is the man waiting for?

A ☐   B ☐   C ☐

3   What is the date of the anniversary dinner?

A ☐   B ☐   C ☐

4 What is the man going to do on holiday?

A

B

C

5 What is the woman having problems with at the moment?

A

B

C

6 What does the girl decide to buy?

A

B

C

7 What does the woman want to do?

A

B

C

Part 2 ▶ 45

Questions 8–13

You will hear part of an interview with a librarian called Sarah Peters about books for English students.
For each question, put a tick (✓) in the correct box.

---

8 What is Sarah talking about?

A	the importance of reading for fun	☐
B	the reason students read in class	☐
C	the need to read when doing homework	☐

9 What does Sarah say is the best way for students to choose a book?

A	It should be part of their course.	☐
B	The topic should attract them.	☐
C	There should be a film of the book.	☐

10 What does Sarah think about books that have been made easier?

A	They are often too hard for students.	☐
B	They are useful for learning new vocabulary.	☐
C	They are a good way of improving different language skills.	☐

11 Sarah recommends *Time Flies* to students because

A	it was written by a famous author.	☐
B	it encourages them to be imaginative.	☐
C	it is like the books they read when they are studying.	☐

12 What does Sarah enjoy most about her job?

A	having contact with students	☐
B	discovering new writers	☐
C	reading travel books	☐

13 What does Sarah think about books in the future?

A	She is sure they will be popular.	☐
B	She is worried about the use of technology.	☐
C	She is pleased that students will use them in their studies.	☐

Part 3 ▶ 46

Questions 14–19

You will hear a holiday guide talking to some holidaymakers about sailing. For each question, fill in the missing information in the numbered space.

Great Sailing holidays

Holiday representative

Holiday reps office is **(14)** .... the hotel reception desk.

Jonas works every evening except **(15)** ....

Meals

Breakfast: 7–10 a.m.

Lunch: Collect food for lunch from the kitchen at **(16)** ....

Dinner: from 7.30 p.m.; self-service

General advice about sailing

Read the leaflet about **(17)** .... before starting.

Make sure you have a lifejacket.

Check the **(18)** .... before leaving.

Take a hat, a bottle of water and some **(19)** .... on the boat.

Part 4 ▶ 47

Questions 20–25

Look at the six sentences for this part.
You will hear a conversation between a girl, Janet, and a boy, Steve, about a television programme
called *Dancing Star*, in which young dancers try to come first and win a prize.
Decide if each sentence is correct or incorrect.
If it is correct, put a tick (✓) in the box under **A** for **YES**.
If it is not correct, put a tick (✓) in the box under **B** for **NO**.

		A YES	B NO
20	Steve wants to know what happened on the latest programme of *Dancing Star*.	☐	☐
21	Janet doesn't like talking about the television programme called *Dancing Star*.	☐	☐
22	Steve says it is difficult to become a professional dancer.	☐	☐
23	Janet thinks it is not a good idea to have programmes like this on television.	☐	☐
24	Steve is worried about what the judges might say to him.	☐	☐
25	Janet thinks that the judges on the programme are not always right in what they say.	☐	☐

Paper 3   Speaking

Part 1

The interlocutor will ask you and your partner some questions about yourselves.

▶ 48 Listen to the recording and answer the questions. Pause the recording after each bleep and give your answer.

Part 2

The interlocutor will ask you and your partner to discuss something together.

▶ 49 Look at the pictures below and listen to the interlocutor's instructions. When you hear the bleep, pause the recording for three minutes and complete the task.

Part 3

The interlocutor will ask you and your partner to talk on your own about a photograph. Your photographs will be on the same topic. Look at the photos on page 112.

▶ 50 Listen to the recording and answer the questions. When you hear the bleep, pause the recording for one minute and answer the question.

Part 4

▶ 51 The interlocutor will ask you and your partner to talk about a topic connected to your photos. Listen to the recording. When you hear the bleep, pause the recording and complete the task.

Answer key

UNIT 1
Grammar

1
1 What is your name?
2 Do you like your name?
3 How did you get your name?
4 How do you spell your name?
5 Would you like a different name?
6 What is your favourite name?

5 1 it 2 can/could/might 3 What 4 How 5 What
1 B 2 A 3 D 4 E 5 C

6
Steve: Hi, I'm Steve.
Bailey: I'm Bailey. Nice to meet you.
Steve: Sorry, I didn't catch that – **what's/what is** your name?
Bailey: Bailey.
Steve: How **do** you spell it?
Bailey: B-A-I-L-E-Y. **Do** you think it's an unusual name?
Steve: Yes! Where **does it** come from?
Bailey: I think it's popular in Australia.
Steve: Have you been there?
Bailey: No, I haven't – it's a long way away!
Steve: So who **gave** you the name?
Bailey: Actually, it was my dad – he just liked it.
Steve: **Do** you have any problems with the name?
Bailey: I think the biggest problem is that it can be a name for both boys and girls.
Steve: Do people find that confusing?
Bailey: Definitely! Before they meet me, they think I'm a boy!

8 1 is his 2 does she come 3 is John
4 did Christine leave 5 she got

Speaking

1
1 Where do you live?
2 How long have you lived there?
3 Do you like living there?
4 Who do you live with?
5 Tell us about your family.
6 Do you work or are you a student?
7 How do you spell your surname?
8 What is your favourite time of day?

2 A 4 B 2 C 3 D 8

5 1 teacher 2 sister 3 study 4 aunt 5 reading
6 cinema

6 1 Where 2 there 3 whether 4 here

Listening

1 1 B 2 C 3 B 4 C 5 C 6 B 7 A

Vocabulary

1 Across
1 shy 4 cheerful 6 punctual 8 generous
10 nervous

Down
2 honest 3 reliable 5 curious 7 ambitious
9 sensitive 11 organised

1 **hair/face:** bald, beard, curly
age: in his twenties, middle-aged, young
looks/appearance: good-looking, handsome, smartly-dressed
size: overweight, thin, well-built

2 A 3 B 1 C 2

4 1 middle-aged, curly, overweight
2 good-looking, bald, thin
3 young, smartly-dressed, beard

Reading

1 1 F 2 H 3 B 4 E 5 D

Vocabulary

1 1 A 2 B 3 B 4 A 5 B 6 A

Grammar

1 1 ✓
2 I'd like to know how you normally meet people.
3 Could you tell me if/whether you use any social networking sites?
4 Can you tell me how you spell your surname?
5 Do you know how the name Mercedes is pronounced in Spanish?

2 1 why you can't 2 why you don't
3 whether/if you are 4 how you feel
5 where you can

Writing

1 D, B, C, A

UNIT 2
Speaking

1 1 frying pan 2 saucepan 3 oven 4 kettle
5 straw 6 hot dog 7 milk shake 8 soft drink

2 1 M 2 M 3 B 4 M 5 W 6 W 7 M 8 M 9 W

3 **Photo 1:** biscuits, bottle of water, bowl, cakes, fork, glass, grass, knife, lake, plate, spoon, table, tablecloth

Photograph 2: apron, bottle of water, cakes, fork, glass, knife, plate, spoon, tablecloth, waiter

4 In the photo I can see a family having a picnic **outside**. They are sitting around a long table which has a **tablecloth** on it. The table is outside near a **lake** and it is on some grass. The weather is good because everyone is wearing summer clothes. There is a lot of food on the table. There are some **cakes** and a bowl of something – I think it's crisps or **biscuits**. There is a big **spoon** in the middle of the table, and plates with food on. On the left there are two little girls who are enjoying the food and they are sitting with their big family. They all look happy.

6 1 B 2 A 3 B 4 C 5 A 6 C

7

	advantage	disadvantage
1	I can eat in the fresh air.	There might be insects. ✓
2	The food is better than the food I cook. ✓	It's expensive.
3	Sandwiches are cheap and easy to prepare. ✓	It might rain.
4	I can cook what I like. ✓	I have to wash up afterwards. ✓
5	I can try new and unusual food. ✓	I might not like the food.
6	I can relax in my own kitchen. ✓	I have to go shopping first.

8

agree	disagree	explain
Me too. ✓	I can't agree.	That's because … ✓
I agree.	I don't agree. ✓	The reason is …
I think the same.	I don't like … at all. ✓	That's why … ✓

Reading

1 1 I wouldn't like to eat a meal like that.
2 There isn't enough food on the plate.
3 Good food should look nice on the plate.

2 1 B 2 D 3 C 4 B 5 A

3 1 ancestors 2 emphasis 3 diet 4 ingredients
5 nutritious 6 Processed

4 1 D 2 A 3 B 4 C

Vocabulary

1 1 washable 2 advertisements 3 careless
4 enjoyable 5 spoonful 6 hopeful
7 careful 8 hopeless

2 1 washful – washable
2 careless – careful
3 armless – armful
4 enjoyable – enjoyment
5 enjoyment – enjoyable

Grammar

1 1 I'm not really enjoying – I don't really enjoy
2 I cook – I'm cooking
3 ✓
4 is weighing – weighs
5 I try – I'm trying
6 I'm not knowing – I don't know

2 Incorrect

3 1 am enjoying 2 get up 3 spend 4 don't have
5 cooks 6 Do you know 7 fry 8 make
9 are trying 10 are only having 11 promise
12 know

4 1 C 2 B 3 C 4 A

Listening

1 1 A 2 B 3 B 4 C 5 A 6 C

2 1 C 2 D 3 A 4 E 5 B

3 1 shopping online 2 scans the products
3 find special deals 4 see the quality (of food)

Grammar

1 1 can't be, must be 2 might rain 3 must be
4 can't be 5 might eat 6 must have

2 1 must be – can't be
2 can't be – must be
3 might be – must be
4 must have – might have, must have – might have
5 must not be – might not be
6 might not be – can't be

Writing

1 1 C 2 A 3 B

2 D, G, A, E, C, F, B

3 1 Just then 2 suddenly
3 A few moments earlier 4 Eventually

4 B, F, D, E, C, I, A, G, H

UNIT 3

Speaking

1 1 T 2 F 3 F 4 T 5 T

2 1 queue 2 supermarket 3 shelves
4 shopping baskets 5 angry 6 casual 7 suit

4 1 C 2 A 3 B 4 E 5 D

5 1 Do you agree 2 I don't get what you mean
3 could you say that again 4 what you mean is
5 go ahead

7 1 B 2 W 3 M 4 B

Vocabulary

1 1 look it up 2 turn their music up 3 get on well
4 give up 5 looking after 6 keep on 7 hurry up
8 cleaning up 9 hand it in 10 hanging out

2 1 amused 2 nervous 3 annoyed 4 excited
5 embarrassed 6 satisfied 7 confident
8 surprised

Listening

1 1 B 2 A 3 A 4 B 5 B 6 B

2 1 I know what you mean. (agree)
2 Good point. (agree)
3 I'm not sure about that. (disagree)

Grammar

1 1 asking 2 to show 3 spending 4 to tell
5 making 6 to stay 7 trying 8 hurting

2 **verb + -ing form:** can't stand, involve, mind, practise
verb + infinitive: arrange, can't wait, expect, learn

3 • … According to research, **having** quality
relationships means …
• If it's difficult **to see** your friends every day or if you
can't wait **to meet** them, you can always arrange
to keep in touch online.
• Friends choose **to love** you for who you are not
what you look like. … To keep a friendship going,
you have to decide **to do** as much as you can for
them too …

Reading

1 1 A 2 A 3 B 4 A 5 A 6 A 7 A 8 A 9 B 10 B

2 1 polite 2 consequences 3 impressed 4 thing
5 circumstances 6 belongings 7 flattered
8 been around

Vocabulary

1 1 B 2 A 3 F 4 D 5 C 6 E

Grammar

1 1 must 2 have to 3 have to 4 have to
5 have to 6 Do you have to 7 should 8 have to
9 should 10 do you have to 11 should
12 have to 13 mustn't

Writing

1 1 T 2 F 3 T 4 T 5 T 6 F

2 Kristian

3 Hi Lucy,
I liked your message. I thought you were very pretty
and intelligent. **W**e can meet next **S**aturday. Club
Seven is good. See you there at eight o'clock.
Stefan

Hi Lucy,
It was great to get your message. I thought you
were really good fun too. That joke you told me was
hilarious**!** How about meeting up next Saturday? We
could go to a movie and then get something to eat.
What do you think?
Kristian

UNIT 4
Reading

1 camels, desert, dry, hot, pyramid, sandy

3 1 E 2 D 3 C 4 A 5 B

4 1 B 2 A 3 D 4 A 5 A 6 C 7 D 8 B 9 C
10 C

5 1 benefited 2 improved 3 orbiting 4 buried

Vocabulary

1 1 Although 2 as well as 3 although 4 also
5 in spite of 6 Despite 7 though 8 too

2 1 in spite of/despite 2 as well as
3 Despite/In spite of 4 although/though
5 However, though 6 also

Grammar

1 1 for 2 for 3 since 4 since 5 for 6 since

2 1 How long have you known your closest friend?
2 How long have you been a student here?
3 How long have you had your mobile phone?
4 How long has your friend had the same hairstyle?
5 How long have you liked your favourite singer?
6 How long have you lived in your house?

4 A came out B haven't made C has decided
D saw E bought, moved F have done

5 1 F 2 B 3 A 4 C 5 D 6 E

Speaking

1 the clothes and the mobile phone

2 1 think 2 about 3 could 4 What 5 Maybe
6 let's

Listening

1 1 guide, shop
2 artist, painting, sculpture
3 catalogue, history
4 exhibit

2 1 C 2 B 3 A 4 C 5 B 6 A 7 A

Grammar

1 1 used to live 2 used to have 3 used to see
4 used to go 5 used to tell 6 used to make

2 1 Didn't you use to go skiing in winter?
2 Yes. We always used to go to Switzerland for two weeks.
3 Did you always use to go in January?
4 Yes. We always used to see the same people there.
5 What did you use to enjoy most?
6 Everything! Falling over was the only thing I didn't use to enjoy./The only thing I didn't use to enjoy was falling over.

3 1 used to get/catch
2 used to wear
3 didn't use to wear
4 used to have
5 used to watch

Vocabulary

1 1 CLIMATE 2 LOCAL 3 GROWTH 4 FRIENDLY
5 FACILITIES 6 NEIGHBOUR 7 ENTERTAINMENT
8 LIVELY

2 1 mild 2 transport 3 facilities 4 fresh 5 spaces
6 playgrounds 7 growth 8 friendly 9 lively
10 going 11 local

Writing

1 1 C 2 B 3 C 4 A 5 B 6 C

2 1 need/have to 2 remembering 3 forgot
4 easier 5 worries

3 1 a modal of obligation 2 an -ing form
3 past simple 4 a comparative 5 present simple

UNIT 5
Vocabulary

1 **Across**
2 jeans 6 jacket 7 trousers 8 skirt

Down
1 tie 3 sweater 4 blouse 5 shirt

2 **Suggested answers (from left to right)**
She's wearing a sweater, trousers/leggings, boots and a scarf.

He's wearing trousers/jeans, a shirt, a sweater, a cardigan and boots.

He's wearing a sweater, trousers/jeans and shoes/trainers.

She's wearing a raincoat, jeans and shoes.

3 1 shirt, blouse 2 tie, scarf 3 overcoat, jacket
4 hat, cap 5 shoes, boots 6 jeans, trousers

4 1 C 2 A 3 B

5 1 old-fashioned 2 up-to-date 3 second-hand

6 1 T 2 T 3 F 4 F 5 T 6 T

7 1 try on 2 go with 3 fit 4 iron
5 put on 6 wear out 7 suit 8 borrow

8 1 goes (well) 2 try on 3 put 4 out 5 fit
6 suits

9 A

10 1 a beautiful blue silk dress
2 my short cotton skirt
3 a horrible red woollen sweater
4 a cheap blue cotton dress
5 a trendy red velvet jacket
6 a smart black leather jacket

Speaking

1 the first photo

2 1 jackets 2 sweaters 3 shelf 4 casual 5 leather

4 1 A 2 A 3 B 4 A

5 1, 3, 4, 7, 9

Listening

1 1 F 2 T

2 1 an age 2 a noun 3 a period of time
4 a noun 5 a noun 6 an amount/a number

3 1 21 2 dogs 3 weekend 4 person 5 park
6 £50

Grammar

1 1 smaller than 2 more independent than
3 noisier than 4 easier, than
5 more affectionate than 6 softer, than

2 Dogs make **the** best pets, in my opinion. They're much more fun **than** cats, rabbits or tortoises. Tortoises have to be the **most** boring pets in the world. My friend has a tortoise and he says they're **more** interesting than I think. They're also a lot **less** expensive to feed than other animals. They're not nearly **as** friendly and affectionate though.

Reading

1 2 Piotr plays the <u>drums</u>. He would like to live with <u>other students</u> with <u>similar interests</u>. He <u>loves animals</u> and <u>would like to have a pet</u>.

3 Lakshmi is studying <u>nursing</u>. She wants to specialise in <u>looking after old people</u>. She <u>loves classical music</u>. She can have her <u>meals at the hospital</u> where she will be working.

4 Anneline <u>needs to be near the university</u> so she can study at weekends. She <u>wants to make new friends</u> while she is in the UK, especially people <u>from other parts of the world</u>.

5 Nourridine is studying to be a <u>chef</u>. He would like to be able to <u>cook his own meals</u>. He plans to bring his <u>car</u> to the UK. He would like to <u>live with an English person</u>.

2 **A** We are a young couple with a <u>baby</u>, a <u>cat</u> and a lovely spare room in our flat. The room has wonderful <u>views of many famous places</u> in London, like Saint Paul's Cathedral. We offer a <u>lower rent</u> to someone who can <u>prepare meals</u> and help <u>look after the baby</u> at weekends.

B My husband and I live with our <u>14-year-old</u> <u>son</u>, Simon, in a beautiful <u>country house</u>. Our other son is studying abroad and we would like to have a student to stay in his room, join us for <u>family meals</u> and also <u>help Simon with his school work</u>.

C There are still <u>shared flats</u> available in our <u>International Student Lodge</u>. You will have access to the <u>library</u> and <u>car park</u> at the university, which is <u>across the road</u>. Students from all over <u>Europe</u>, <u>Asia</u>, <u>Africa</u> and <u>America</u> have made Student Lodge their home. Why not join them?

D I am offering <u>free accommodation</u> in exchange <u>for help with my mother</u>, who is now almost <u>90</u>. You will have your own room but I'm afraid I <u>cannot</u> <u>provide meals or let you use the kitchen</u>. I have a <u>season ticket for the opera</u>, which you are welcome to borrow from time to time.

E I'm looking for someone to <u>share my flat</u> with me. I'm a 22-year-old boy <u>from Manchester</u>. You will have your <u>own room</u>, use of the <u>garage</u> and <u>access to the kitchen and laundry</u>. <u>No pets or</u> <u>smokers</u>, I'm afraid.

F We have a room to rent in our house. There are <u>three</u> of us <u>sharing</u>. I'm from <u>Sweden</u>, Julio's from <u>Argentina</u> and Eddie, the <u>dog</u>, is from England! We are keen <u>guitarists</u> and we <u>play together</u> most evenings. I mean, Julio and I play; Eddie sometimes sings!

3 **1** A **2** F **3** D **4** C **5** E

Vocabulary

1 **1** garage **2** curtains **3** carpet **4** chimney **5** fan **6** duvet

2 **1** antique **2** balcony **3** garden **4** air conditioning **5** blinds **6** pillows

Grammar

1 **1** Nicolas always wears such smart clothes.
2 Most performance cars are too expensive for someone like me.
3 I didn't know it was such a small country.
4 I'm not hungry enough to eat a whole pizza!
5 We were so tired that we went straight to bed.
6 There are not enough open spaces for children to play in my town.

2 **1** such **2** so **3** such **4** so **5** such **6** so

Writing

1 say why you have decided to live there

2 **Suggested answer**
I chose this family because they live near the centre of London.

3 **1** T **2** F **3** T **4** T **5** T

UNIT 6
Reading

1 A

2 **1** A **2** C **3** D **4** C **5** D

3 **1** slopes **2** upset **3** balance **4** grassy **5** embarrassing **6** lowered

4 **1** give up **2** Get up **3** getting on **4** give away

Vocabulary

1 **1** At first **2** in fact **3** in the end **4** because of **5** at all **6** at least **7** up to date **8** on sale

Grammar

1 **1** C **2** A **3** B

2 **1** practised – was practising
2 studied – was studying **3** was moving – moved
4 spoke – was speaking **5** was passing – passed
6 was calling – called **7** was laughing – laughed
8 learnt – was learning **9** walked – was walking
10 wasn't understanding – didn't understand

3 **1** went **2** left **3** was worrying **4** were **5** met
6 was talking **7** discovered **8** didn't know
9 cycled **10** bought **11** was raining **12** joined

Vocabulary

1 **1** teacher, project **2** homework
3 lecture hall, lecturer **4** course, research
5 report **6** curriculum **7** modules **8** seminar

2
1 easyer – easier, efort – effort
2 concantrate – concentrate   3 progres – progress
4 rejister – register, evning – evening
5 atend – attend, truble – trouble   6 cleer – clear

3
1 originally   2 continually   3 easily   4 basically
5 broadly   6 clearly   7 hard   8 considerably

4
1 The students looked very confused and obviously didn't understand the teacher.
2 Students have to work hard to finish their course.
3 The new computer room is great but, unfortunately, it's just for older students./The new computer room is great but it's just for older students, unfortunately.
4 My friend can speak French well.
5 The lesson was clearly too difficult for most of the students in the class./Clearly, the lesson was too difficult for most of the students in the class.
6 There is one student in my class who is continually talking/who is talking continually – the teacher gets very cross.

Listening

1   1 C   2 D   3 E   4 B   5 A

2   1 gets   2 found   3 passed   4 deal with   5 spent
6 taking

3   parking, theory test, cyclists

4   1 B   2 B   3 B   4 A   5 A   6 A

Speaking

1   3 and 4

2   A

3   1 Well   2 I mean   3 As a matter of fact
4 you know   5 Mind you   6 Well, you know
7 Anyway   8 I like

Grammar

1   1 got   2 had told   3 felt   4 had missed
5 didn't know   6 got   7 had already given out
8 hadn't had   9 didn't feel   10 seemed
11 had barely looked   12 saw   13 had written
14 said   15 had only answered   16 was
17 had failed   18 came out   19 saw   20 had got

2   1 By the time I woke up, I had missed my doctor's appointment.
2 As soon as Adam had collected his luggage, he went to look for a taxi.
3 When Heather had finished doing her homework, she went out.
4 After we had done the shopping, we came home and cleaned the house.
5 By the time Christine got to the beach, it had started to rain.

6 As soon as he had blown out the candles on the birthday cake, he started opening his presents.
7 By the time Stephen finished his breakfast, his sister had left for school.
8 When the teacher arrived, the students had already stopped talking.

Writing

1 and **2**

It was my first day. My mother **had hung** my new school uniform in the wardrobe the night before. She **had put** my new school shoes next to the chest of drawers.

The next morning, after I **had had** my shower, I started to get dressed. Suddenly, I realised that my school shoes **weren't** there. It was only then that I remembered that I had left my bedroom door open the night before.

I ran downstairs and out into the back garden. There was our new puppy, Eddie, with one of my new school shoes in his mouth! He **had already destroyed** the other shoe.

3   Suggested answers
A
1 It was my first day at university.
2 I was feeling a little bit anxious but also curious about the other students, the lecturers and the course.
3 In fact, something rather strange had happened a few days before.
4 I had been looking at clothes in a shop I really like when I saw a boy I know trying to steal a leather jacket.
5 I decided to call out his name and he was so embarrassed that he put the jacket back.
6 I was still thinking about what had happened when I realised that the lecturer was asking me a question.
7 I tried to remember the last thing I had heard her say but my mind was a complete blank.
8 Finally, I decided to admit that I hadn't been listening.
9 We finished the lecture and she smiled at me as she went out of the room.
B
1 It was my first day in a completely new job.
2 I was feeling nervous because I'd never had a proper job before.
3 In fact, something rather strange had happened the night before.
4 I had been in bed for about an hour when I heard someone outside the house calling out my name.
5 I decided to ignore it and soon after I fell asleep.
6 I was still thinking about what had happened when I saw the boss standing in front of my desk.
7 I tried to pretend I had been thinking about the latest sales figures but I don't think he believed me.

8 Finally, I asked him a question about the company and he seemed to be pleased about that.

9 We went on talking about company policy for the next 20 minutes or so.

C

1 It was my first day on holiday with my friends.

2 I was feeling really great because I knew we were going to have a really fantastic time.

3 In fact, something rather strange had happened exactly a year before.

4 I had been on my way to the airport when I realised I had left my passport at home.

5 I decided not to go and get it because I knew I could travel on my national ID.

6 I was still thinking about what had happened when I realised that I had left my small backpack at home with all my favourite clothes in it.

7 I tried to phone my mother but I didn't have enough credit on my phone to make an international call.

8 Finally, I managed to send her a text message and she promised to post it to me the next day.

9 We went to the post office every day for a week but the backpack never arrived.

UNIT 7
Listening

1 1 C 2 D 3 F 4 E 5 A 6 B

2 1 C 2 B 3 B 4 B 5 A 6 C

Grammar

1 **countable:** book, kilometre, language, lesson, raindrop, snowflake
uncountable: advice, frost, rain, smoke, snow, steam
both: coffee, glass, noise

2 1 Many 2 a lot of 3 much 4 Few 5 a lot of
6 much

3 1 noises 2 glass 3 glasses 4 bread 5 paintings
6 noise

Vocabulary

1 **Across**
2 snow 8 thunderstorm 9 shower 11 chilly
12 gales

Down
1 frost 3 wind 4 pour 5 wet 6 sunshine
7 freezing 10 fog

2 1 fog 2 thunderstorm 3 frost 4 sunshine
5 gales 6 pouring

Speaking

1 1 F 2 T

2 1 M 2 M 3 M 4 A

3 1 agree 2 Why 3 think 4 How about 5 What
6 right

4 1 A 2 F 3 E 4 D 5 B 6 C

Reading

1 1 C 2 H 3 D 4 G 5 A 6 E 7 B 8 F

2 1 B 2 A 3 B 4 B 5 A 6 B 7 B 8 A 9 B 10 B

3 1 useful pieces of advice 2 take quickly
3 protection 4 cold 5 fussy 6 make it feel better

Vocabulary

1 1 E 2 A 3 I 4 C 5 G 6 B 7 D 8 F 9 J 10 H

2 1 ✓ 2 amazed for – amazed by
3 keen about – keen on 4 tired with – tired of
5 ✓ 6 interested for – interested in
7 familiar on – familiar with
8 involved about – involved in/with 9 ✓
10 fond with – fond of

Grammar

1 1 advice 2 a thunderstorm, the noise 3 Glass
4 smoke, fire 5 bread 6 The coffee
7 water, the tap 8 cheese, milk

2 1 – 2 – 3 the 4 The 5 – 6 – 7 a 8 an
9 The 10 the 11 a 12 – 13 The 14 –
15 the 16 the

3 We had **a wonderful time** in **Egypt**. As you know, we took **a cruise** down **the Nile**. We started in **Cairo**. **The boat** was really luxurious and **the itinerary** was amazing. We saw all **the most famous** archaeological sites like **the Pyramids of Giza** and **the Valley of the Kings**. **The guides** were great and **the other people** on **the boat** were good fun. I tried to learn **a bit** of **Arabic** but everyone spoke good English. On **the last night** there was **a special party** with **fantastic food** and **wonderful music**. By **the time** we got to **bed**, **the sun** had already come up!

Writing

1 **A** 2 **B** 1/9 **C** 3 **D** 5/8 **E** 4 **F** 6 **G** 8/5 **H** 9/1 **I** 7

2 You were right. We got back from the **cruise** last week. It was great.

We sailed from Barcelona to **the** Balearic Islands of Menorca, Mallorca, Ibiza and Formentera. Formentera was the best part for me. There is **a** fantastic hippy market there and I **bought** some really cool earrings and some sandals. There **were** really nice people on board the ship and lots of games and competitions. I'm not very keen on that kind of thing though. I prefer to just lie on deck and look at **the** sea.

Well, that's all my news. Write soon and **tell** me when you are coming to visit us.

UNIT 8
Vocabulary
1 dress, glamorous, shoes

2 1 C 2 E 3 F 4 A 5 H 6 G 7 D 8 B 9 I

3 1 chat show 2 ballet dancer 3 rock star
4 stadium concert 5 stage actor 6 soap operas
7 television commercials 8 magazine covers
9 designer clothes

Speaking
1 the first photo

2 1 In 2 In 3 On 4 in 5 On 6 At

5 Yes, they did.

6 Yes, they did.

7 1 I'm not so keen on (him). 2 I bet you like (her).
3 I used to be (really) into (Cody Simpson).
4 You can't beat (a good boy band).
5 I don't mind (her). 6 I can't stand (Justin Bieber).

Reading
1 A

2 1 C 2 D 3 A 4 B 5 A 6 D 7 B 8 C
9 A 10 D

3 role model media outlet charity worker

4 1 ideal 2 worthwhile 3 talent 4 depressing
5 escape 6 glamorous 7 trend 8 achievement

Vocabulary
1 1 -ed 2 -ing

2 1 depressing 2 fascinated 3 surprising 4 bored
5 interesting 6 encouraging 7 amazed
8 worrying

3 1 depressed 2 fascinating 3 encouraged
4 interested 5 boring 6 frightening 7 surprised
8 worried

4 1 fascinated – fascinating 2 depressed – depressing
3 ✓ 4 ✓ 5 interesting – interested 6 ✓
7 frightening – frightened 8 ✓

Grammar
1 1 (that) he had seen Mylie Cyrus in an airport once.
2 (that) he had met Emma Watson in a café in March.
3 (that) she didn't believe him though.
4 (that) he had never met anyone famous.
5 (that) he was always saying that he had seen someone famous somewhere or other.
6 (that) she had been to the Academy Awards ceremony a couple of times.
7 (that) it had been amazing.
8 (that) she couldn't go this/that year because there was something really important she had to do that day.
9 (that) she would tell me if she was going (the) next/following year.
10 (that) I could join her.

2 1 ✓
2 She told me (that)/She said (that) she didn't like having her photo taken.
3 She told me (that)/She said (that) she would be at home on Saturday night.
4 ✓
5 ✓
6 Carla told us (that)/Carla said (that) she had tried to get a part in a movie.
7 ✓
8 Luke told me (that)/Luke said (that) he would be late for the interview.
9 She told me (that)/She said (that) she was going home.
10 ✓

3 1 'I can speak Japanese.'
2 'I don't like having my photo taken.'
3 'I'll be at home on Saturday night.'
4 'You have to practise more.'
5 'I don't want to be on a TV show.'
6 'I tried to get a part in a movie.'
7 'You can borrow my camera.'
8 'I'll be late for the interview.'
9 'I'm going home.'
10 'I was late for school yesterday.'

4 1 had grown up 2 had always surfed 3 had surfed
4 knew 5 had always loved 6 had (only) started
7 had never (really) shown 8 wanted

Listening
2 1 F 2 F 3 T

3 1 twenty-one/21 2 smile 3 clothes 4 Spanish
5 photograph 6 24/24th/twenty-fourth

Grammar

1
1 He asked me if/whether I found Brad Pit attractive.
2 He asked me what I liked most about him.
3 He asked me if/whether I thought he was more attractive than Johnny Depp.
4 He asked me what I had thought of his latest film.
5 He asked me if/whether Angelina Jolie was/had been in it too.
6 He asked me who else was/had been in it.
7 He asked me if/whether I had seen any of her films.
8 He asked me if/whether I was going to the cinema that weekend.
9 He asked me if/whether he could come with me.
10 He asked me how much the tickets would cost.

2
1 She asked me where I lived.
2 She asked me if/whether I had always lived there.
3 ✓
4 She also asked me what I was studying at the moment.
5 ✓
6 ✓
7 She asked if/whether I had got any special plans for the future.
8 She wanted to know what I was going to do when I finished studying.
9 ✓
10 She wanted to know if/whether I enjoyed watching television or listening to music.

Writing

1 Story A: 1, 2, 5
Story B: 2, 3, 4

UNIT 9
Speaking

1 1 F 2 T 3 T 4 F

2 1 T 2 T 3 F 4 T

3 Creative thinking: explore, many solutions, search
Critical thinking: analyse, logic, one solution

4 1 C 2 F 3 B 4 E 5 D 6 A

5 1 there, front 2 artist 3 wearing, beard
4 what, looks 5 middle, like 6 background
7 is, so 8 side, what

Grammar

1 1 can, can't 2 Can 3 managed to
4 couldn't 5 managed to 6 Will you be able to

2 1 be 2 could 3 to 4 manage 5 can 6 not

3 1 able 2 can 3 can/will/would 4 could
5 could 6 can't 7 be 8 can/will

Reading

1 1 A 2 C 3 G 4 H 5 F

2 1 outfit 2 stuck 3 studio 4 techniques
5 trouble 6 materials

Vocabulary

1 1 tried 2 plans 3 good (at) 4 needed
5 shown 6 finish

2
1 Sonia is not a very good sculptor but she's very good at paining.
2 She has shown her work all over Europe and Asia.
3 She needed a visa for some of the countries she visited.
4 I tried to enrol in a course at the art college but my application arrived too late.
5 I hope to finish my studies early next year.
6 I planned to study painting and drawing.

3 1 would like, let us know 2 departs 3 further
4 completed 5 request 6 provides students with

Listening

1 1 E 2 D 3 B 4 C 5 F 6 A

2 1 B 2 C 3 C 4 B 5 A 6 A

Grammar

1 1 who 2 who 3 who 4 that 5 who 6 that
7 which 8 which

2
1 Joseph Conrad, who is one of the world's greatest writers in English, was not a native speaker of that language.
2 His father, who had translated Shakespeare's plays into Polish, died when Joseph was only 11.
3 Joseph then lived with his uncle, who was a very careful man.
4 However he let the boy, who was only 16 at the time, go away to sea.
5 His experiences on board ships, which sailed to countries like India, Africa and Australia, inspired many of his novels.

3
1 My friend Stephanie, who I met in France, is from the north of England.
2 To celebrate her birthday, which is next week, we are all going out for lunch.
3 Then we are all going to see an exhibition at a gallery where they always have fantastic exhibitions.
4 The artist whose paintings we are going to see is called David Hockney.

5 His paintings, which are so big they cover whole walls, are mainly of the north of England.

6 After the end of May, when the exhibition finishes, it will only be possible to see the paintings in New York.

Vocabulary

1 **1** job, careful **2** long **3** uniform **4** training **5** kinds, records **6** listening to **7** fashionable **8** studied

2 **1** firefighter **2** scientist **3** teacher

3 **1** teamwork **2** problem solving **3** communication skills

4 **1** not **2** not **3** again **4** not **5** not **6** personal

5 **1** unhappy **2** disagree **3** unwell **4** irregular **5** unemployment **6** dislike **7** uninteresting **8** impossible **9** impatient **10** disadvantage

6 **1** impatient **2** dislike **3** unwell **4** self-employed **5** retrain **6** impossible **7** irregular **8** unhappy

Writing

1 (that) working **2** expected to **3** unless **4** is necessary **5** as

UNIT 10
Listening

1 **1** identity **2** golden **3** pounds **4** laptops **5** newspaper **6** convenient **7** viewing **8** discounts **9** bargain **10** Saturday

2 **1** Golden **2** 2 **3** Laptops **4** 9 **5** identity **6** newspaper

Grammar

1 **1** B **2** B

2 **1** T **2** no information **3** no information **4** T **5** F **6** T

3 has it never been used, is shaped, is tempted, have been placed, are protected, can be stored, can be brought back, can be plugged into, is equipped, can't be carried around, was made

4 **1** Many people see advertisements before they buy a product.
  2 Designers present their spring and summer fashions in Fashion Weeks in London, Paris and Milan.
  3 Make-up artists and hair stylists help models with their make-up and hair.
  4 The person who stole the jewels put them on sale last week.
  5 A famous Italian model designed the spring collection.
  6 Somebody else has already worn this jacket.

5 **1** are often advertised **2** is bought **3** is checked **4** were sold **5** are found **6** was sold **7** have been pulled **8** were given **9** are sometimes made **10** was being advertised

Vocabulary

1 **1** G **2** B **3** A **4** D **5** H **6** E **7** F **8** C

2 **1** boutique **2** computer store **3** baker('s) **4** newsagent('s) **5** supermarket **6** department stores

3 **1** baker('s) **2** florist('s) **3** chemist('s) **4** supermarket **5** computer store **6** furniture store **7** butcher('s) **8** jeweller's

4 **1** C **2** H **3** E **4** A **5** F **6** B **7** D **8** G

Grammar

1 **1** had my hair cut
  2 are having our building repainted
  3 is having his jeans mended
  4 had her toenails painted bright green
  5 are having our windows cleaned
  6 had my computer fixed
  7 has his/her shoes made
  8 have my car repaired

2 **1** Where do you get your hair cut?
  2 How often do you get your car serviced?
  3 Why did you get a tattoo done?
  4 How old were you when you got your ears pierced?
  5 When did you get your teeth whitened?
  6 Where did you get that shirt made?
  7 How often do you get your eyes tested?
  8 When did she have her portrait painted?

3 **1** G **2** E **3** C **4** D **5** A **6** B **7** F **8** H

Reading

1 **1** C **2** C **3** A **4** B **5** A

2 **1** receipt **2** charge **3** period **4** maintenance **5** valid **6** facilities

3 **1** facilities **2** charge **3** maintenance **4** valid **5** receipt **6** period

Vocabulary

1 **1** about **2** for **3** for **4** from **5** about **6** on **7** in **8** for

2 **1** planning for – planning to
  2 listen at – listen to
  3 complains on – complains about
  4 arguing of – arguing about
  5 planning to – planning on
  6 lent my book for – lent my book to

7 told my friend for – told my friend about
8 argue to – argue with

3 **1** on **2** of **3** for **4** from **5** about **6** about
7 for **8** to

Speaking

1 **1** T **2** F **3** F **4** T **5** T **6** T **7** F **8** T

2 **1** definitely **2** think **3** something **4** right
5 not **6** point

3 **1** If I wanted **to** sell …
2 The goods are usually **sent** …
3 That's what I've **been** told.
4 You could **be** right.
5 It might get **damaged**.
6 That's **a** good point.
7 A friend of **mine** …
8 He **makes** quite a lot …

Writing

1 **1** B **2** A

2 Dear Patrick,
Thank you very/so much for the book. I am going to start reading it as soon as I finish studying for my exams.
Bye for now,
Tania

Hi Patrick,
I've just opened the parcel with the book you sent. I love fantasy novels, as you know. I've already started reading it. It's absolutely fantastic!
Love,
Fabiola

3 **Suggested answers**
1 I have always wanted to read a story set in your country.
2 Thank you so much.

4 Dear James,
Thank you for sending me the book, which I enjoyed very much. I would like to send you a gift in return because I was so pleased. What are your favourite things? Please tell me so I can send you something.
Bye,
Carla

UNIT 11
Reading

1 F

2 **1** D **2** C **3** B **4** B **5** A

3 **1** confused **2** embarrassed **3** irritating **4** likely
5 greeted

Vocabulary

1 **1** C **2** F **3** H **4** A **5** B **6** G **7** D **8** E

2 **1** old-age, old-time
2 self-assured, self-confident
3 hand-painted, hand-sewn
4 well-/badly-paid, well-/badly-written

3 **1** old-age **2** self-service **3** one-way
4 hand-painted **5** well-paid

4

j	m	p	g	t	h	s	o	u	v	e	n	i	r	s	e
w	c	a	p	a	t	o	s	q	b	k	c	e	w	j	w
d	w	h	p	h	o	v	l	x	a	y	g	n	a	o	i
e	k	q	g	s	o	m	m	i	p	e	j	r	a	u	k
s	r	i	n	e	p	u	o	s	d	m	l	u	x	r	j
p	l	h	o	t	e	l	s	q	q	a	a	o	m	n	m
f	d	o	l	v	b	y	v	b	k	h	y	j	z	e	p
g	u	i	d	e	b	o	o	k	s	n	h	i	x	y	x

5 **1** flights **2** hotels **3** guidebooks **4** journey
5 souvenirs **6** maps **7** holiday

6 **1** exchange rate **2** live webcams
3 take photographs

7 **1** D **2** C **3** A **4** B

8 **1** setting off **2** ended up **3** look for **4** get rid of
5 set up **6** turned into

Listening

1 **1** A **2** C **3** B **4** B **5** C **6** C **7** A

Grammar

1 **1** will get on, will like
2 are you meeting, are meeting, are having
3 will have to, will get
4 am going to study, am going to take, am going to visit

2 **1** are you going to do
2 does your plane leave
3 is going to rain
4 I have, I'll probably study
5 Are you having, I'm just going to have

6 starts
7 are you going to do
8 I'm having, are meeting
9 does the lesson start
10 you'll have

Speaking

1 Candidate 1: the third photo
Candidate 2: the second photo

2 1 T   2 F   3 F   4 T

3 Yasmina: **in** the foreground, **in** the background, **on** the left

Fatima: **on** their right, **in** the background, **in** the top right-hand corner

Grammar

1 1 will   2 am going to   3 will   4 will
5 are going to   6 will   7 are you going to
8 am not going to   9 am going to   10 will

2 1 I**'ll help** you with them.
2 ✓
3 Naira has decided that she **isn't going to get** a dog after all.
4 He**'s going to wear** them to the party tonight.
5 ✓
6 ✓
7 He**'s going to have** his hair cut.
8 ✓

Writing

1 B

2 1 At first   2 You know how   3 But   4 too
5 Let me know   6 All the best

UNIT 12
Grammar

1 1 C   2 E   3 A   4 B   5 F   6 D

2 1 If I don't have anything to do on Saturday mornings, I have breakfast in a café.
2 If I have a match, I have something quick at home.
3 I walk to the park if it's a nice day.
4 If it's raining, my friend drives me.
5 The coach tells us off for playing badly if we lose.
6 If we win, he takes us all out for a pizza.

3 1 You'll never swim fast **unless you practise/if you don't practise** a lot.
2 I**'ll tell** you if I decide to take that climbing course.
3 If we **miss** the last train, we'll have to walk home.

4 Unless you **work** hard, you won't be successful.
5 You**'ll feel** very proud if you get to the top of the mountain.
6 If you ask me to do something, I**'ll do** it for you.

4 1 E   2 C   3 B   4 F   5 A   6 D

5 1 get   2 look   3 speak   4 will roll   5 gets
6 treat   7 respond/will respond   8 stop
9 will change

Listening

1 1 A   2 B   3 B   4 B   5 A   6 A

2 1 don't get, give up   2 get, criticise
3 manage, will go   4 do you talk, are
5 do you go, want   6 is, will spend   7 do, will climb
8 do you feel, don't get   9 are, will give up
10 stops, won't go out

Reading

1 1 A   2 A   3 B   4 A   5 B

2 1 B   2 A   3 A   4 B   5 B

3 1 welcome   2 delayed   3 approaching
4 recommended   5 Unfortunately   6 dangerous

Vocabulary

1 1 remember   2 take   3 trips   4 bring
5 reminding   6 come   7 go   8 travel

2 1 work   2 lend   3 miss   4 stay   5 losing   6 live
7 job   8 learn   9 borrow   10 teach

Grammar

1 1 If I were bitten by a poisonous spider, I **would** go straight to the hospital.
2 If I **saw** a big vicious dog coming towards me, I would run away.
3 ✓
4 ✓
5 If I saw a shark while I was swimming, I **would** try to swim away.
6 If a bear **came** up to me while I was hiking in the woods, I would try to frighten it away.

2 A would walk   B would lie   C would tell
D would stand   E would hit   F would put

3 1 F   2 D   3 A   4 C   5 E   6 B

4 A 6   B 1   C 2   D 5   E 4   F 3

5 1 would   2 could   3 would   4 was/were
5 would   6 would

Speaking

1 1 P 2 M 3 P 4 P

2 1 You **could** eat the chocolate bar if you were hungry.
2 If the cigarette lighter didn't work, the candle **would not be** any good.
3 We **wouldn't** have any time to draw pictures if we were lost!

3 1 were/got, would 2 have, got 3 had, would
4 sent, would

Vocabulary

1 1 C 2 J 3 G 4 F 5 D 6 B 7 I 8 A 9 E 10 H

2 1 athletics 2 surfing 3 tennis 4 hiking

3 1 enter, prize ✓ 2 instructor ✓, join in
3 train, fitness 4 experienced ✓, safety
5 practice ✓, compete

4 1 did 2 played 3 goes 4 play 5 do
6 playing 7 go 8 go 9 doing 10 play
11 go 12 doing

Writing

1 between 2 the most 3 so (that) 4 winning
5 more than

VOCABULARY BANK
Using a dictionary

1 A 6 B 2 C 7 D 4 E 1 F 5 G 3 H 8

2 1 important 2 choice 3 little 4 except
5 record (n)

3 1 include 2 verb 3 yes 4 2 5 exclude
6 in 7 long 8 second 9 yes
10 no; the verb is transitive – it needs an object.

Collocations

1 1 on 2 in 3 at 4 out of 5 by 6 for

2 1 pieces 2 stock, stock 3 time 4 private
5 least 6 the same time 7 hand 8 order
9 foot 10 board 11 a long time 12 a reason

3 1 of 2 about 3 at 4 for 5 to 6 with

4 1 brilliant/good at 2 jealous of 3 bored with
4 suitable for 5 proud of 6 polite to
7 responsible for 8 late for 9 angry with
10 terrible/bad at 11 grateful for
12 worried about

5 1 for 2 from 3 on 4 to 5 of 6 at

6 1 take care of 2 borrow, from 3 recover from
4 depends on 5 approve of 6 concentrate on
7 remind, of 8 replied to 9 waiting for
10 belongs to 11 stay at 12 arrive at

7 1 take 2 make 3 have 4 do

8 1 had 2 saving 3 make 4 perform 5 keeping
6 run 7 break 8 print 9 gain 10 pay
11 doing 12 give

Word formation

1 1 im- 2 ir- 3 un- 4 dis-

2 1 B 2 D 3 A 4 C

3 1 dis- 2 self- 3 re- 4 im- 5 mini- 6 non-
7 re- 8 un-

5 1 -y 2 -ly 3 -able 4 -less 5 -ful 6 -ment

6 actor, artist, builder, designer, director, farmer,
instructor, journalist, photographer, reporter, sailor,
scientist

7 1 acceptable 2 foggy 3 designer 4 actor
5 loudly 6 disagreement 7 pleasurable
8 careless 9 patiently 10 disappointment

9 1 B 2 F 3 A 4 D 5 H 6 C 7 E 8 G

10 1 show business 2 signpost 3 music festival
4 hard disk 5 railway line 6 exchange visit
7 information pack 8 snowstorm

11 1 F 2 A 3 B 4 H 5 G 6 E 7 D 8 C

12 1 never-ending 2 broken-hearted 3 two-hour
4 one-way 5 long-distance 6 world-famous
7 energy-efficient 8 home-made

Phrasal verbs

1 1 E 2 B 3 H 4 G 5 D 6 A 7 F 8 C

2 1 look up 2 give up 3 bring up 4 hang up

3 1 G 2 B 3 A 4 E 5 H 6 F 7 C 8 D

4 1 get on 2 get on with 3 keeps on 4 carried on

5 1 F 2 G 3 C 4 A 5 D 6 B 7 H 8 E

6 1 went off 2 worn off 3 set off 4 put, off

7 1 C 2 F 3 D 4 A 5 H 6 E 7 G 8 B

8 1 going out 2 set out 3 handed out
4 run out of

9 1 B 2 H 3 F 4 A 5 C 6 D 7 E 8 G

10 1 look after 2 looking forward to 3 call in on
4 thrown, away

Different meanings of get

1 buy 2 receive 3 improve 4 arrive 5 move
6 find 7 become 8 prepare

Easily confused words

1 packet   2 sensible   3 foreigners   4 advice   5 told
6 opinion   7 scenery   8 remind   9 lend   10 bring

Same sound, different spelling

1 except   2 there   3 hear   4 weather   5 see
6 Where

COMMON ERRORS: PRELIMINARY

1
1 **What's** your name?
2 Where **are** you from?
3 What **do** you do?
4 Where **are** you going?
5 How many times **have** you been outside your country?
6 What **did** you enjoy most about the experience?

2
1 Would you mind telling me **how I get** to the station from here?
2 Can you tell me when **the microscope was** invented?
3 I'd like to know **if you enjoyed** the party.
4 Could you tell me **what you find** easiest about learning English?
5 I'd like to know **whether I am** allowed to have friends come to stay.
6 Would you mind telling me **how you spell** your surname?

3
1 People who **live** in glass houses shouldn't throw stones.
2 My sister **rides** her bicycle to college every day.
3 When **are** you coming to visit us again?
4 I **am going** away for the weekend so I'll be a bit late on Monday.
5 My brother **doesn't** like hip hop music.
6 You **take** the tram to La Laguna. It **stops** opposite the university.

4
1 He **must be** exhausted. The match has been going on for over five hours.
2 It **can't** be the postman. He never comes this early.
3 I'll answer the phone if you like. It **may/might/could** be for me.
4 We **can meet** on Wednesday or Thursday. I don't mind.
5 Take an umbrella, just in case. It **may/might/could** rain later.
6 When I finish college, I **might go** and work in another country.

5
1 If you ask me, **buying** a new computer is a waste of money.
2 She apologised for **arriving** late.

3 I'm better at **watching** tennis than I am at **playing** it.
4 Would you mind **passing** the salt?
5 We're looking forward to **hearing** about your holiday in Greece.
6 We've arranged **to meet** outside the cinema at 5.30.

6
1 You **must not walk** on the grass.
2 I **have** to go. See you later.
3 **Do we have** to buy a book or is the teacher going to give us photocopies?
4 If you want to lose weight, you **shouldn't** eat so many cakes and sweets.
5 **Should I wear** a hat to the wedding?
6 Sue won't be here next Tuesday. She **has to** go to the dentist.

7
1 **Have you ever been** to Paris?
2 Yes, several times. In fact, I **went** last November.
3 A friend of mine **went** last year. He says it's very expensive.
4 Well, it used to be but this time I **found** it quite cheap.
5 Where **did you stay**?
6 In a little hotel near the Sorbonne. It**'s been** there for ages. My great-grandfather **used to stay/stayed** there every time he **went** to Paris.

8
1 We had **such a** good time at the party.
2 Susan is **such a** nice person.
3 This tiramisu is **so** delicious! Can I have some more?
4 You're not **old enough** to stay out after midnight.
5 Snowboarding is **such/so much** fun. I love it.
6 I'm afraid the exam was (**much**) **too difficult** for me. I don't think I'll pass.

9
1 as/so good at   2 a better   3 the worst
4 worse than

10
1 Where **did** your father live when he was a child?
2 Who **won** the Eurovision song contest last year?
3 We all **felt** ill after the meal.
4 I fell in love with Fernando the first time I **saw** him.
5 We **bought** Mum some perfume for her birthday.
6 I **caught** a terrible cold while I was in London.

11
1 Alex **was listening** to some music on his phone while the teacher was telling us what to do for homework.
2 Some of the contestants were rehearsing when the stage **collapsed**.
3 I was phoning my friend on her mobile when I **saw** her standing on the corner.
4 You were sitting there watching the match while I **was cooking** the dinner!
5 I **was having** a shower when the telephone rang.
6 Tim **was sleeping** soundly while the burglars were stealing his new flat-screen TV.

12
1 As soon as I **got** to school, I remembered that the teacher had told us there was going to be an exam that day.

2 I felt really nervous because I **had missed** lots of lectures.

3 By the time I got to the classroom, the teacher **had** already started the exam.

4 I had hardly looked at the questions when I **saw** that the boy sitting next to me had written almost a whole page.

5 When the teacher **told** us to stop writing, I had only answered two of the three questions.

6 I was sure I **had failed** but, in fact, in the end I got quite a good mark.

13 **1** She was wearing **trousers** and a jacket.

2 Are we having **chicken** for dinner again?

3 She's got **lovely** dark curly hair.

4 How **much** money do you spend on food and entertainment each week?

5 There **is too much furniture** in this room.

14 **1** I love living here because **the** sun shines almost every day.

2 There's **a** volcano here that is almost 4,000 metres high.

3 I prefer living on **the** coast to living in **the** countryside though.

4 It's wonderful to be able to swim in **the** sea every day.

5 There's also **a** lake near here which has very clear water.

6 I sometimes go there at night and swim in the light of **the** moon.

15 **1** She **told me**/She **said** that she would be a little bit late.

2 I **told the neighbours** that I was going to be away for a few days.

3 Tim **said** that he would be home on Saturday night.

4 Tanya said that she **couldn't** ride a bicycle.

5 Paulo told me he **was** coming on Monday.

6 Gustave said he **would** be here by midday but he still hasn't arrived.

16 **1** She asked me how **I was** feeling.

2 She asked us **if/whether we enjoyed** our English course.

3 She asked me **if/whether I had** any special plans for the future.

4 She asked me what **I was going** to do when I finished university.

5 She asked me **if/whether there was** anything special I **wanted** to do in the future.

6 She asked me what kinds of things **I liked** doing in my spare time.

17 **1** I can understand the news on the radio now but I **couldn't** even understand my teacher a few months ago.

2 I **can** read short books in English now but I couldn't even read a newspaper at the beginning of the course.

3 I **am able to/can** write stories, reports and articles in English now but I **couldn't even /wasn't even able to** write an informal letter when we started using this book.

4 I can express my opinion in English now but I **couldn't** even talk about a photo properly last September.

5 I **can** pronounce most words quite well now but I **couldn't** even understand the pronunciation symbols in the dictionary at the beginning of the course.

18 **1** Tina, **who** came to your party, is living in Paris now.

2 Thor Heyerdahl, **who** died in 2000, discovered some pyramids on the island of Tenerife.

3 She's the girl I told you about.

4 Tim's the boy **whose** father is a politician.

5 Is Fabio the boy **who/that** is going to France next year?

19 **1** Oh no! I think I'm **going to be** sick.

2 I have to go now. I**'ll** phone you back later.

3 What **are you going to do** next year when you finish school?

4 What time **does** your plane leave?

5 Look at those dark clouds. It **is going to rain** later.

6 I've already decided. I**'m going to buy** Ella a CD for her birthday.

20 **1** How **do you feel** if you don't get enough sleep?/ How would you feel if you **didn't get** enough sleep?

2 What would you say if you **met** someone famous?

3 Who do you usually talk to when you **are** worried about something?

4 How **would** you feel if Australia won the World Cup?

5 What **will you do** this summer if you can't afford to go on holiday?

6 What would you buy if you **had** £100,000?

21 **1** My boyfriend is quite well-**built**. He's medium-**height** (about 1.80) and a little bit **overweight** but I still think he's very **handsome**. The thing I like most about him though is that he is always very **honest**.

2 You'll love our house in the mountains. In the winter, when it's been snowing outside, we all sit around the **fire** and talk after dinner. It's so cosy. It can be quite hot in summer but, luckily, we have **air-conditioning** so we keep nice and cool. I hope you can come next year.

3 The person in my family I get **on** with best is my older sister. We're really good friends. She's about seven years older than me so she looked **after** me and my younger brother a lot when we were little.

4 I couldn't work **out** the meaning of a word and I decided to **look it up** in a dictionary. It wasn't there so I looked **for** it online but I couldn't find it there either. In the end I gave **up** and decided to ask the teacher.

5 A lot of people criticise it but I get a lot of **enjoyment** from watching television. I even like the **advertisements**.

6 I wanted to buy a new top because **of** the hot weather. There were some nice ones **on** sale **in** a shop near here. I tried one **on** but I wasn't very keen **on** the way it looked **on** me. I'm really tired **of** looking **for** clothes that fit me. I never find anything!

EXAM STRATEGIES
Reading and Writing (Paper 1)

1 1 C 2 A 3 B

2 The student forgot advice 2 .
The correct answer is C.

3 1 B 2 A 3 C

4 The film is only partly a match for Sue. It is a true story and has a happy ending, which match Sue's needs, but it is a musical, which she doesn't want. The student forgot Advice 2.

5 1 synonyms 2 exactly 3 different

6 It is false because there is a 'chance to relax' if wanted, although the afternoon is full of activities.

7 1 writer's purpose 2 opinions and feelings 3 before

8 1 and 3

9 1 T 2 T 3 T

10 1 D (2) 2 B (1) 3 D (3)

11 **A** as close as possible **B** no more than **C** must

12 1 C 2 A 3 B

13 1 You **have to** write about all three points in the task.
2 You should **not** write more than 45 words.
3 You **can't** write fewer than 35 words.

14 1 and 2: The candidate has missed the last point and written more than 45 words.

15 1 B 2 B 3 B 4 B 5 L 6 S

16 The candidate has forgotten 2, 3 and 6.

Listening (Paper 2)

1 1 C 2 A 3 B

2 1 B 2 C 3 A

3 B

4 1 opinion(s), attitude(s) 2 agree(s) 3 different

Speaking (Paper 3)

1 3 and 4

2 3

3 2

4 2 and 3

PRACTICE TEST
Paper 1: Reading

Part 1

1 B 2 A 3 C 4 C 5 C

Part 2

6 G 7 D 8 C 9 F 10 A

Part 3

11 A 12 B 13 B 14 A 15 B 16 A 17 A 18 A 19 B 20 B

Part 4

21 C 22 A 23 A 24 B 25 B

Part 5

26 A 27 C 28 D 29 B 30 A 31 B 32 A 33 C 34 D 35 C

Paper 1: Writing

Part 1

1 for 2 surprised by 3 better than 4 had 5 rained

Paper 2: Listening

Part 1

1 C 2 C 3 B 4 B 5 C 6 A 7 C

Part 2

8 A 9 B 10 C 11 B 12 B 13 A

Part 3

14 next to 15 Wednesday 16 9 (a.m.)
17 safety/staying safe (on the water) 18 weather
19 sun cream

Part 4

20 B 21 B 22 A 23 B 24 A 25 A

Audio scripts

Unit 1, Grammar Activity 7

Track 02

Steve: Hi, I'm Steve.

Bailey: I'm Bailey. Nice to meet you.

Steve: Sorry, I didn't catch that – what's your name?

Bailey: Bailey.

Steve: How do you spell it?

Bailey: B-A-I-L-E-Y. Do you think it's an unusual name?

Steve: Yes! Where does it come from?

Bailey: I think it's popular in Australia.

Steve: Have you been there?

Bailey: No, I haven't – it's a long way away!

Steve: So who gave you the name?

Bailey: Actually, it was my dad – he just liked it.

Steve: Do you have any problems with the name?

Bailey: I think the biggest problem is that it can be a name for both boys and girls.

Steve: Do people find that confusing?

Bailey: Definitely! Before they meet me, they think I'm a boy!

Unit 1, Speaking Activity 3

Track 03

Examiner: How long have you lived there?

Candidate 1: About three years – we moved there when my dad changed his job.

Examiner: Do you like living there?

Candidate 1: It's a nice place – there are lots of things to do, like playing tennis.

Examiner: Who do you live with?

Candidate 2: My mother, father and two brothers, who are older than me.

Examiner: What is your favourite time of day?

Candidate 2: The morning when it's sunny and the birds are singing.

Unit 1, Speaking Activity 5

Track 04

1	teacher	4	aunt
2	sister	5	reading
3	study	6	cinema

Unit 1, Listening Activity 1

Track 05

1 **Which picture shows the girl's brother?**

   A: Have you seen the pictures of my brother I uploaded to my photo page?

   B: I don't know what he looks like – does he have fair hair like you?

   A: Not at all – he's got dark curly hair and he's quite thin – he used to be fatter but he lost a lot of weight when he started playing tennis every week. He wears glasses for reading but not every day – and he's not wearing them on the Facebook photo.

2 **How did the man find out about the football result?**

   A: Did you find out about the football? I couldn't see it in today's newspaper.

   B: No, it was an evening game and it went into extra time so it finished too late for the morning papers. I had hoped to listen to the whole commentary on the radio but I couldn't get good reception. Luckily, there was a report on the late night news on television so I was able to see the goals too.

3 **What will the weather be like at the weekend?**

The weather has been unsettled lately, with temperatures lower than normal for the time of year. Even so, some places have had plenty of sunshine today, though the sun hasn't really warmed the air much. However, that's all set to change. Tonight rain will move in to the north, where there might even be some light snow showers as temperatures drop, although if there is snow, it will melt quickly. The rain will be heavy in all areas and looks set to continue until Saturday – probably Sunday as well. So wear warm clothes and don't forget the umbrella!

4 **Where will the man go first?**

   A: Why are you leaving so early? Your haircut is not until 11.30.

   B: I know, but I have to go to the bank. I need to pay a bill. And while I'm in town, I can take those library books back – that will save us having to pay a fine because they're late! But I must get some petrol before anything else, otherwise we'll run out and I won't go anywhere!

   A: Could you please stop at the post office and get some stamps? I want to write some letters tonight.

   B: OK. I'll have to do that after my haircut though.

5 What did the girl buy for Julia's birthday?

A: Did you get something for Julia's birthday? I've got her a new pen.

B: I looked everywhere and couldn't make up my mind. I almost bought her a necklace but it was very expensive – especially as there were matching earrings too. Then I remembered that she needs gloves, and there was this good deal in one shop with a scarf too – so I got them both. Next year I'll have to get her something different though. Maybe just a good book – she likes reading.

6 Which television programme does the man want to watch?

A: What do you want to watch on television tonight? There's a great concert – that new girl singer's going to be on.

B: I'm not in the right mood for that – I want something more exciting. I'd quite like to give that new science fiction series a try – you know, the one we recorded last week. I suppose we could watch that documentary about formula one racing – though it doesn't start until ten and I'm quite tired.

7 What will the woman wear to the theatre?

A: I need some advice! You know I'm going to the theatre tomorrow night – I can't decide what to wear. I've got that smart suit with the short skirt and jacket but it's a bit like a work outfit.

B: What about that long skirt? You've got that new cardigan I bought you to go with it.

A: It's a bit summery. It's still cold so I'd have to wear a jacket with it. I think it'll have to be the suit. I like wearing trousers but I don't think they're really suitable for the theatre.

B: Whatever you feel comfortable in!

Unit 1, Vocabulary Activity 3

Track 06

1 My friend Janet is middle-aged. She's got very pretty curly hair. She's a bit overweight so she's always worrying about what she eats.

2 Nick is very good-looking, in my opinion. He's almost completely bald but that makes him even more handsome. He's quite thin, I suppose, but I find that very attractive too.

3 Tim is quite young. He's probably in his early twenties but he's always very smartly-dressed. Over the last couple of months he's grown a beard. I think it really suits him.

Unit 2, Speaking Activity 2

Track 07

A: Hi, Sally. How are you doing?

B: Fine, thanks. I'm looking forward to eating with you on Saturday!

A: Yes! I love food that I've cooked myself – I use really fresh ingredients and I try to cook healthy food. I think it's really tasty then, and I know what goes into the food. I love health food restaurants though. I often eat at one of those.

B: I'm not good at cooking myself. I'd rather eat out in restaurants. I love choosing interesting food from a long menu!

A: I prefer eating stir-fry vegetables because I don't like fatty food. In fact, I don't eat much meat at all although I'm not a vegetarian. I do like chicken and other white meat.

B: Oh, I'm the opposite. I love meat, burgers and chips – things like that. I know it's not good for me and maybe I should go on a diet. If it's green, I don't like it! I'm not really so keen on chicken either.

A: Well, there's a local speciality I make with fish and boiled rice. You'd love that, I'm sure – and it won't make you fat!

B: I don't really like fish – that's a problem! Although I could try it, I suppose.

A: You'll like it the way I make it – even I hate raw fish! You'll see on Saturday evening – I'll cook for you then. You'll love it!

B: Thanks! But remember: I don't like wine. I prefer soft drinks.

A: No problem! I only drink plain water myself.

B: And not too many green things!

Unit 2, Speaking Activity 5

Track 08

In the photo I can see a family having a picnic outside. They are sitting around a long table which has a tablecloth on it. The table is outside near a lake and it is on some grass. The weather is good because everyone is wearing summer clothes. There is a lot of food on the table. There are some cakes and a bowl of something – I think it's crisps or biscuits. There is a big spoon in the middle of the table, and plates with food on. On the left there are two little girls who are enjoying the food and they are sitting with their big family. They all look happy.

Unit 2, Speaking Activity 7

Track 09

A: I love eating outside. A picnic in the park or by a lake is just great. That's because the food is easy to prepare – I usually take sandwiches – and cheap too.

B: I don't agree. There might be lots of insects and I don't like them! That's why I prefer to eat in a restaurant. I can try different food that I've never tasted before, and it's much better than my cooking!

A: Me too. But I quite like eating at home too. I can cook what I like to eat and relax afterwards.

B: I don't like eating at home at all – I have to wash up afterwards! That's too much work for me and as I said, I'm not a very good cook.

Unit 2, Listening Activity 1

Track 10

Interviewer: Today we're talking to Chris Jones, a successful young chef who has just begun a career in television. Chris, tell us why you decided to become a chef in the first place.

Chris: I've always loved cooking. When I was very young, I spent a lot of time in the kitchen watching my mother prepare meals – she helped me a lot. When I was at school, my friends laughed at me. They were all doing things like sport and they thought that cooking was for girls! Although my teachers said it was a crazy idea, I was determined and went to college to study nutrition.

Interviewer: After college you decided to open your own restaurant. Why was that?

Chris: When I finished college, I went to work in a restaurant in France – that was because I wanted to get as much experience as possible – and I learned a lot. The chef there taught me to cook his own special dishes, which gave me ideas for my own recipes. I wanted to share my ideas for food with other people and that was what made me start my own restaurant. I didn't really care about the money but it's quite nice to work for myself.

Interviewer: What's your favourite food?

Chris: When I was a child, I loved the things my mother cooked – typical food like cakes and sausages. But learning about nutrition at college got me interested in unusual combinations of tastes and now I love creating different healthy salads. Top of my list though is fish; there are so many different things you can do with it and it's easy to create new recipes.

Interviewer: Then you started working in television. How did you feel about doing that?

Chris: It was strange, really. By chance, a TV producer came into my restaurant. He liked my food, we started talking and he said that he was looking for a chef to do a new series of cooking programmes. I went to the studio for an audition. There were other chefs there and I was amazed when they offered me the job.

Interviewer: How did you feel before the first programme?

Chris: Good question! We spent a lot of time practising everything before the first programme and it was all very exciting. There was a lot for me to remember though, and I was nervous in case the food wasn't good. You see, I was cooking the food during the programme, which was live, not recorded, and if anything had gone wrong, I would have been very embarrassed.

Interviewer: You're very successful now and you're very young. How do you see the future?

Chris: There are so many different things I want to do! There may be a new television series but I will definitely write a book – that's a good way to get people to try my recipes so it's top of my list. I will keep my restaurant, of course, and I might open some more, though that's not a priority. And it would be great to travel so that I can try food from all over the world. But first things first!

Unit 3, Speaking Activity 3

Track 11

I can see five people standing in a long queue. They are in a supermarket because they have all been shopping and there are lots of shelves with food on. They are all carrying shopping baskets with things in that they want to buy, and they have to pay the cashier. I think they have been waiting a long time because they look a little bit angry! All the people are wearing casual summer clothes except the last man, who is wearing a smart suit. He must be on his way home from work.

Unit 3, Speaking Activity 6

Track 12

A: I hate waiting in queues when I'm in a hurry – you know, like when I've got up late or something and I have to wait in a queue to buy a ticket. Do you agree?

B: Yes, I do! And I hate queuing when someone at the front is taking a long time and doesn't seem to understand that there are other people waiting.

A: Sorry, I don't get what you mean.

B: Well, what I mean is they have no awareness of other people – they are just selfish.

A: But maybe they have a difficult problem. What I hate is when there are not enough people dealing with customers – you know, not enough checkouts open – that sort of thing.

B: Sorry, could you say that again?

A: Not enough checkouts open – that sort of thing.

B: So what you mean is there should be more checkouts, that it's the shop's fault that there is a queue.

A: Exactly! I don't mind queuing when I have someone to talk to or when I have plenty of time or when …

B: Sorry, can I say something?

A: Sure, go ahead.

B: OK … I don't mind queuing when I know there's a good reason. I hate it when I'm in a traffic jam though.

A: I agree!

Unit 3, Listening Activity 1

Track 13

Peter: This looks like a great restaurant. Shall we try it?

Carol: My friend's been here and said it was nice. The chef is pretty good and the prices are reasonable. Let's try it.

Peter: There's a free table over there by the window.

Carol: OK. So now for the menu. I hope they won't take too long as I have to be back for a meeting in an hour.

Peter: I thought it was this morning?

Carol: It was but then it was rearranged for later this afternoon. I might have forgotten to tell you. I'm sorry that I have to hurry.

Peter: I see. No, I must have got it wrong myself. I probably wrote it down in the wrong place in the diary!

Carol: Oh look, they do a fish pie! That's one of my favourites and it takes so long to cook at home. Not that I do it very much – I'm not fond of cooking.

Peter: I know what you mean!

Carol: And there's meat pie too. Now I don't know what to choose!

Peter: Well, I'm not very hungry so I'll go for the salad. I know it'll be nice and healthy.

Carol: Good point. And maybe the fish pie will take too long for them to prepare. OK, I'll have salad too. Though it's not very exciting!

Peter: I don't get what you mean – it's delicious and very good for you! You should try different dressings, like olive oil. They make all the difference.

Carol: I'm not sure about that. It always tastes like salad to me! But it *is* convenient just now.

Peter: So shall I call the waiter? Excuse me …

Unit 3, Grammar Activity 2

Track 14

A: Are you going to that speed dating event on Saturday?

B: I can't go this weekend after all but I want to go the following weekend. I must remember to tell them I want to change the day.

A: Can you do that?

B: Yes, basically. But you have to tell them four days in advance and you also have to pay €5 extra.

A: Perhaps I could go this weekend in your place.

B: No, I'm afraid that's not possible. You have to be registered with FastDate and you're not a girl!

A: Oh! So if someone takes your place, they have to be the same sex as you? Tell me more about it. Do you have to wear special clothes?

B: No, but everyone wants to make a good impression so you should try and look your best. I usually wear jeans and a smart jacket.

A: How long do you get to talk to each person?

B: Five minutes. Then a bell rings and you have to move to the next table. That should be enough time to decide if you might want to see that person again.

A: What happens if you run out of things to say?

B: Well, it's a good idea to prepare some questions in advance, just in case, but not too many – you should try to be natural and spontaneous.

A: If you like someone, what do you have to do next?

B: After each conversation you put a tick next to the person's name if you want to see them again. I think you should try and make a few notes as well to help you remember the person. Then, the next day, you have to go to the FastDate website and enter your ticks online. If the other person has ticked you too, you get each other's contact details so you can arrange a date.

A: It sounds great! You mustn't forget to email me the website address so I can register too.

Unit 4, Speaking Activity 1

Track 15

A: Well, the capsule doesn't look very big so, do you think we should choose small things?

B: Maybe. But the clothes would be a really good way of showing what people wear today. Don't you agree?

A: Definitely, but I think the fashion magazine would show what we look like now. I mean, not just the clothes we wear but also hairstyles, jewellery and make-up.

B: Actually, I think you're probably right. And the magazine will take up less space in the capsule.

A: How about the mobile phone? We could put lots of different kinds of music on it, and photos and videos as well.

B: Yeah, maybe. But the technology will be very different a hundred years from now. They might not be able to use it.

A: Hmm … you could be right. And the battery will have run out, of course! What do you think about the money?

B: I'd definitely put that in. After all, it doesn't take up much space and it will be interesting for people to see the images and writing on the coins and notes. How about the newspaper?

A: It's a bit big. Maybe we could just use the front page. They'd know what the main news stories were that day.

B: Hmm … yeah, good idea. Then we could fit the recipe in as well. That would tell them about what kinds of food we eat.

A: And I love Spaghetti Carbonara! So let's put the fashion magazine, the money, the front page of the newspaper and the recipe in our capsule. Whoops! We forgot something.

B: Oh yes – the photo of the city. We can put that in as well if you like.

A: Agreed. Cities probably will have changed a lot by 2116!

Unit 4, Listening Activity 1

Track 16

1 guide, shop
2 artist, painting, sculpture
3 catalogue, history
4 exhibit

Unit 4, Listening Activity 2

Track 17

1 Where is the art gallery?

A: Excuse me, can you tell me where the art gallery is, please?

B: Of course. Just keep going along this road until you get to the traffic lights at the crossroads. There's a big department store on the left on this side of the lights, and a museum just past the lights on the same side of the road. The art gallery is opposite the museum, on the right.

A: Thanks very much.

2 What did the woman like best in the museum?

A: It's a great museum. I thought those old bowls were fascinating! They had beautiful shapes painted on them – it must have taken ages to do that!

B: That's true but I quite liked the costumes from 200 years ago. It's interesting that people were shorter then, and the dresses were lovely.

A: Yes, I agree about that.

B: But for me it was the jewellery section that was most interesting – I could have stayed there all day!

3 When is the best day for students to visit the museum?

The museum is open from nine to five every day except Sundays, when it is closed. There is a 20 percent discount for anyone over 65 on Tuesdays, and anyone at school or college can get in for free on Wednesday if they show their identity card. On all other days they have to pay full price. Family tickets are available on Saturdays, when children under 12 are free if they come with two adults.

4 What did the man buy in the museum shop?

A: So what did you buy?

B: Well, I wanted to get a mug – you know, one of those with a picture of something from the museum on it, like a vase, but they only had black ones left and I didn't like them. I decided that a key-ring with a picture of the museum on it was the best thing to get, although I nearly bought a pen because there

was this beautiful silver one in an old style. But it was a bit expensive and I didn't want to spend too much.

5 What does the girl say is most useful to her?

A: What are you doing?

B: I'm planning my English homework. I've got to write about the thing that is most useful in my life. I'm not sure what to say. I use my laptop for work and also chatting to friends but I don't take it everywhere with me. It's too big!

A: I think you have to say a dictionary. After all, it is English homework!

B: That's true. And I suppose most people will write about their mobile phones. Yes, I think that's a good idea – thanks!

6 What has the boy kept the longest?

A: I've been tidying up my room. It's great to throw things away sometimes.

B: Yes. But isn't it difficult to throw away things that have happy memories? I've got lots of things that I want to keep. Like, I have a ticket from my first visit to the theatre last year and a teddy bear that belonged to my mother – that must be the oldest thing I have. I keep a photograph of my grandmother on my wall but that was only taken a couple of years ago so it's not very old. But I wouldn't want to lose any of them!

7 Where does the woman want to go at the weekend?

A: What shall we do on Saturday?

B: Good question! We went to the art gallery last weekend, which was great – I really enjoyed that. What about the museum? I hear it's got some new exhibits that would be interesting. And it's free too! Or there's that new film at the cinema. Though it didn't get very good reviews so let's not go and see that.

Unit 5, Vocabulary Activity 6

Track 18

Helen: Hi, Joe! I didn't expect to find you in the shopping centre. I thought you hated buying clothes!

Joe: Hi, Helen. Oh, I do! It's a complete waste of time as far as I'm concerned! But my sister's getting married next month and I have to get some formal clothes to wear. I'm not doing very well though. I tried to borrow some from a friend but they didn't fit me.

Helen: Shall I help? I've got a few minutes to spare and I'm always happy to talk about clothes! I want to work in fashion if I can so I may have some ideas for you.

Joe: That would be great! I know that I have to get a suit. That's not too bad – I can do that – but choosing a shirt and tie is a nightmare! I have loads of jeans and T-shirts but I never wear smart clothes like that so I don't know where to start.

Helen: Colour's the important thing – they have to go together. What's your favourite colour?

Joe: I have no idea. Blue, I suppose.

Helen: Great! That's easy – that goes with most other colours. A good thing you didn't say orange or purple – that would be much more difficult! What about a dark blue suit, a white shirt and a light blue striped tie?

Joe: Is that boring? It sounds rather old-fashioned to me and I don't want anyone to think I'm not up-to-date in what I wear.

Helen: Well, it's not exactly trendy! But as it's for a wedding, I think it would be a safe choice and you would look nice.

Joe: Well, thanks. Would you like to come to the shop with me and help me choose?

Helen: Sorry, I've haven't got time right now. But if you haven't managed to find anything by next Saturday, I'll come with you then. I'm going shopping with my friend anyway so helping you won't take long. There's a great second-hand shop that sells really good stuff. You might get something cheap there. And if you don't wear formal clothes very often, that might be a good idea.

Joe: Sounds great!

Unit 5, Speaking Activity 1

Track 19

I can see two people who are shopping together. They are both wearing casual clothes and are having a good time. One girl is carrying a lot of bags – she has bought a lot of new things already! She is carrying a big handbag on her shoulder. The other girl has a handbag too, and they are both looking in a shop window at some boots and shoes. One girl is pointing at a pair she likes – maybe she will buy them.

Unit 5, Speaking Activity 3

Track 20

I can see two people shopping for clothes. They are talking and looking at the clothes in a shop. They can see some jackets hanging up and some sweaters that are folded on a shelf. I can see price tags but I don't know how much the clothes are. They are both wearing casual clothes. One of the men is wearing a leather jacket. They are interested in buying something new to wear.

Unit 5, Speaking Activity 4

Track 21

A: So, we have to talk about clothes we wear every day and clothes we wear when we go out. Do you have any ideas?

B: Well, that's an interesting question! I work in an office so I have to look smart, though I often have to wear a dark suit – you know, a jacket and skirt. I have lots of different ones and different coloured blouses to go with them. I take a lot of time to make sure the colours go together. I think that's important. How about you?

A: Hmm … I don't have the same problem as my wardrobe is not very full! I hate shopping for clothes so I only have a few – that rather limits what I can wear every day. What do you think about going out? Do you think that's important?

B: Well, it's good to feel that you look nice. I don't worry about it but I do enjoy going out shopping with friends to buy really nice clothes – something special. I have lots of really nice evening clothes! What do you think?

A: Actually, I don't agree with you at all. If people like me, then it doesn't matter what I wear when I'm out with friends. I have more important things to think about than what I'm wearing! Do you think I'm right?

B: Not at all!

Unit 5, Listening Activity 3

Track 22

Do you love animals but have no time to look after one full-time? Do you spend all your time earning money, which is still not enough for you to keep a pet? Here's the answer: join our Pet Share Club and rent a pet! You must be over 21 to join but the perfect age is over 25. We even have members up to 75! You will need to prove your age by showing your identity card when you register with the club.

We have all sorts of pets to rent: rabbits, cats and so on – but dogs are the favourites.

Once you have joined, we give you a card, which you must show every time you rent a pet. You can take a pet home for a day, a week or even a month – it's up to you but the majority of our members find a weekend is best. Every time you want to rent a pet, you need to make a booking. You can do this on the website, by phone, in a text or in person, which is the best and fastest way.

We try to match new members with a pet we think suits their personality but we also encourage them to choose an animal that is a good size for their home. It's not a good idea to choose a large animal if you live in a small flat, no matter how sweet it is! And it's important that you are able to give the animal enough exercise so although you don't need a big garden, you need to have a large park close to your home.

So how much does it cost? There's a monthly payment of £25 on top of the annual membership fee of £50. There's also a charge for every time you rent a pet; that's £20 at weekends or £12 on weekdays.

Why not give us a try? You'll love it! And you can rent a pet as often as you like. It could change your life!

Unit 6, Listening Activity 3

Track 23

George: How are the driving lessons going, Janet? I'm finding it pretty hard-going. I just seem to get one thing right when something else goes wrong.

Janet: I know what you mean! My driving instructor is great though – she's very patient. I think I would get very stressed if she got cross with me.

George: Hmm … mine isn't so kind. He tends to go on at me and talks when I'm trying to concentrate.

Janet: I found the theory of driving pretty easy. I passed that without any problems. But it's very different when you have to drive the car and deal with all the other traffic on the road as well! Cyclists are very difficult – they seem to do what they like and it's not always easy to see them.

George: I don't have a problem with that. I'm very aware of cyclists as I actually cycle a lot myself and I know you have to be careful. And although I had to spend a lot of time studying for the theory test, I passed it, though only just!

Janet: So what do you find the most difficult? For me it's parking. I know it's a bit of a joke that women can't park a car but I always get worried about it. I never know where the end of the car is.

George: I'm learning in a small car so that's pretty straightforward. I think in my case, it's starting on a hill. It's so hard the engine keeps stopping, which is horrible! I always feel that people are laughing at me.

Janet: When's your actual driving test?

George: Oh, I've got a couple of months yet – plenty of time to get my confidence up.

Janet: Yes, me too. Though I'm not sure that I'll be ready. I feel as though I have a long way to go. And the lessons are *so* expensive! I may have to wait a while before I take it because I want to pass first time.

Unit 6, Speaking Activity 1

Track 24

Examiner: Sofia, do you work or are you a student?

Sofia: I'm a student.

Examiner: What do you study?

Sofia: Well, I've just finished studying at an art school but I would like to go on studying. I mean, I want to study something else, like Master's degree.

Examiner: Xin, are you a student too or do you work?

Xin: As a matter of fact, I work *and* I study. I work, you know, part-time in a café but I'm studying as well.

Examiner: What do you study?

Xin: Medicine. I work in the evening and study in the morning and afternoon. Mind you, it can be a bit difficult at times. I don't have much spare time.

Examiner: What do you enjoy doing with your friends?

Xin: Well, you know, the normal things that young people like to do. Sometimes we go to a club or to the cinema. Anyway, we enjoy just being together.

Examiner: And, Sofia, what do you enjoy doing with your friends?

Sofia: Well, the same things as Xin, really. I mean, I like going to clubs or maybe going round to a friend's house for a meal.

Unit 7, Listening Activity 2

Track 25

Interviewer: Today we're talking to Nadia Winters, who is the youngest weather presenter on television at the moment. Nadia, were you always interested in science and the weather at school?

Nadia: Well, I was always fascinated by the weather and I loved geography as well, although some types of science, like biology, were not my favourites. I had to do science, though, because I wanted to have a job connected with the weather. On the other hand, I was also pretty good at drama at school.

Interviewer: Did you always want to work in television?

Nadia: I not only wanted to work in television, I actually wanted to be a weather presenter. According to my parents, I used to watch the news on television in the evenings with my parents and I used to turn the sound off, turn the subtitles on and read the weather forecast from that. I was never worried about performing in front of other people.

Interviewer: Was it easy to get your first job on television?

Nadia: I studied media at college but I knew it would not be easy to get a job in the television industry. I started out working very long hours behind the cameras but I was lucky when one weather presenter went to work for another television channel and I was given the chance to try the job. It was a challenge but I knew it was the right thing for me and I did my best. Luckily, I was good at it!

Interviewer: What is the best thing about the job you are doing now?

Nadia: There are lots of things I love about it: I get to travel a lot, which is great, and I meet so many people – I think that's the biggest thrill for me. Of course, it's fun to be famous but that can be difficult too – I can't go shopping without people speaking to me.

Interviewer: Do you need any special skills to be a television weather presenter?

Nadia: I studied drama, which definitely influenced me at first. Everyone starts trying to act while they're presenting. But then I realised I couldn't think about acting at the same time as I was giving detailed information. The key is confidence, which comes from just being yourself. People watch me to find out what the weather is going to be like. I don't get too technical because people generally just want to know what clothes to wear that day!

Interviewer: How easy is it to give correct details in your forecasts?

Nadia: The further forward we go, the less accurate our forecast is. Everyone says, 'When I was younger, the summers were so much better,' but last summer wasn't bad and the rain we had in June was very much needed because April and most of March were completely dry. Personally, I love windy weather – it feels so dramatic!

Interviewer: Nadia, thank you! And let's hope we have a hot and sunny summer this year!

Unit 7, Speaking Activity 2

Track 26

Ana: Well, I think all these places would be good for a disaster movie except the beach. What do you think?

Martin: I think the first place with the river and the waterfall could be a good choice. The people in the canoe could be trying to get away from some kind of danger.

Ana: Hmm … What about the other settings?

Martin: And the fishing boat in the storm reminds me of a movie I saw but perhaps the director could make, like, a second one. You know, *Storm at Sea II* or something like that.

Ana: Yes, I saw that film too.

Martin: So I think the best choice is the storm.

Ana: I suppose so but what about the surf beach?

Martin: No, the storm at sea is my favourite.

Unit 8, Speaking Activity 4

Track 27

In the middle of the photo there is a celebrity but she doesn't look very happy. In the background there are lots of people, men and women, who are all trying to take photographs of the celebrity and she doesn't like it. She is trying to get into a car. On the left-hand side of the photo I can see a lot of cameras. The photographers are pushing each other because they are rushing to get a picture. On the right-hand side of the photo I can see a woman taking photographs of the celebrity with her mobile phone. At the top of the photo there is a building – I think the celebrity has just left this building.

Unit 8, Listening Activity 2

Track 28

We're looking for people to appear on our reality TV show. It's completely new – no one will be put in a house and watched, do any strange tasks or live in the jungle. In fact, you'll interview celebrities to find out about their lives, although they won't know you're coming! That's the fun part!

We don't want anyone who is nervous or shy but we want outgoing people with good communication skills. The minimum age is 18 and the maximum 24, although we will consider others outside these limits if they are suitable. Ideally, people will be around 21.

We don't expect anyone to have any television experience as the point of the programme is ordinary people asking questions that celebrities will not expect. We give training on presenting techniques, like not staring into the cameras and how to speak and smile naturally. We also help with things like hairstyles and make-up, and we provide clothes for the presenter – we want to bring out their personality because that makes the programme lively and interesting.

One thing that's absolutely necessary is the ability to speak other languages because many celebrities come from other countries – Italian and French are useful, although Spanish is the top priority.

Send an email with your phone number and one photograph. The address is on the programme's website, although you can't apply directly there. Don't send any more information at this stage. We will call you back and invite you for an audition. You must apply by 15 April as we will be interviewing from 23 to 24 April, and will choose successful applicants by 25 April. Training starts on 30 April and filming begins on 1 June. It's a very exciting project and we hope lots of people will apply!

Unit 9, Speaking Activity 2

Track 29

In this talk I'm going to compare two types of thinking: critical thinking and creative thinking. By 'creative thinking' I mean being able to think of new ideas from old ones. It's important to understand this because of what happens in schools. Teachers often concentrate on critical thinking and teach their students to analyse and make a logical argument. This means that they only think of one correct solution. This is a useful skill but people who can also use creative thinking are able to think about different ideas and look for many possible right answers and not just one 'correct' one. Does this matter? Yes, because although creative thinking is not often taught in schools, in the real world both kinds of thinking often work well together.

To show you what I mean, here is an example: imagine there is a problem that needs to be solved. How should we do it? First, we should look at the problem, think of several possible solutions and then choose the best one. After that we can decide whether it was the right thing to do or not. You can see that in this way we are able to use both kinds of thinking together to help us find the perfect solution to the problem.

Unit 9, Speaking Activity 6

Track 30

A: In the middle of the photograph there's a man sitting in front of a painting. I think he's an artist. He's wearing a T-shirt and a baseball cap, and he has a beard. I can't see what the painting is but it looks like a lot of lines and strange shapes.

B: In the middle of the photo there's a woman holding something – it looks like a fish. In the background there are some other strange things – maybe she made them herself. She's wearing jeans and a sweater, and she's smiling, so I think she's happy. On the right-hand side there's a plant but I don't know what it's called.

Unit 9, Listening Activity 2

Track 31

Interviewer: Brian, why did you become a computer games designer?

Brian: I grew up playing games, though my family weren't keen – I played with friends. I studied computer graphics and animation at college. That course taught me so much about how to make things look realistic, which fascinated me. But I couldn't get a job in game design immediately. I had to work in an office but after a while, I got a job in a local games company.

Interviewer: What is most difficult about your job?

Brian: It can be hard to get a new idea, especially on your own. It's easier to work in a team, sharing ideas, but that has its own problems: trying to explain your thoughts to other people, for example. For me though, it's keeping going when things go wrong – I don't want to give up.

Interviewer: What do you enjoy most about your job?

Brian: Creating something new that people want to play is satisfying. I love the process, from coming up with an idea to seeing it happen. And if the game also looks good, that's great. The best thing though is when I see people enjoying games I've worked on – that makes me feel good.

Interviewer: You worked on *Village Games*, didn't you?

Brian: Yes. That was the most complicated game so far. I wanted players to create their own story while they were playing. Those kinds of games are very popular but they're difficult to design. With *Village Games* it was also hard to make it challenging but not impossible so that people felt frustrated and stopped playing. Players have to feel they have achieved something.

Interviewer: Do you think children should be encouraged to play computer games?

Brian: I believe they are really useful because they encourage children to think creatively. In future that might help to find answers to world problems like global warming and over-eating. Some parents think they are a waste of time though! I have to say that not all children like them – there are plenty who prefer sport because it's more physical.

Interviewer: What makes a good games designer?

Brian: It's not so vital to be a player although most designers are. It's good to have an idea of people's personalities so that you can create realistic characters in your games. In my opinion though, the best developers are able to be patient and to understand how long it really takes to produce a great game.

Interviewer: Thank you for talking to us, Brian.

Unit 9, Vocabulary Activity 2

Track 32

1 I have to work well with my colleagues – what we do is dangerous, and so we depend on each other. Trusting the team is the most important thing and it's that aspect of the job that I like best. We also have to pay great attention to detail, as if things go wrong – like the water not coming through or the hose not working properly – then we can't do our job.

2 I love doing the research and coming up with new ideas that can change things for the future – especially in medicine. I work in a laboratory most of the time and although there's a team of us working on the same project, I do tend to do experiments on my own. That means I don't need leadership skills but I do need to be good at problem solving, which I really like.

3 I have to manage so many different things in a day – it's not easy dealing with a lot of children all at the same time! It's vital to have good communication skills because if they understand why you want to do something, they are more likely to enjoy it. I get such a feeling of satisfaction when the class understands what they are learning!

Unit 10, Listening Activity 1

Track 33

1 identity
2 golden
3 pounds
4 laptops
5 newspaper
6 convenient
7 viewing
8 discounts
9 bargain
10 Saturday

Unit 10, Listening Activity 2

Track 34

OK, now here's some information about the special sale taking place in the town next Saturday evening. Unfortunately, there's been a change of venue: it was originally planned to take place in the Cross Keys Hotel but it's been moved to the Golden Hotel in the town centre as this is a more convenient location for everyone. There is parking at the hotel for £5, although anyone who doesn't mind a short walk can save money and park for £2 on the common.

There are lots of exciting and interesting things for sale, all at amazing discounts. Some examples of items for sale include televisions, stereos and best of all, laptops at 50 percent off! They will be sold very quickly so don't miss out! Everything will be available for viewing on Friday evening from seven to eight, but make sure you get here early on Saturday as it's a case of first come – first served! The doors open at nine and the sale finishes at four.

There are extra discounts for people over 65 so remember to bring your identity cards with you – and everyone must bring their credit card for purchases!

We will all benefit from this sale as ten percent of all profits will be given to the local wildlife sanctuary. So come along and support the sale. You can help the town and get a bargain for yourself! If you want to know more, then look on our website, localradio.com, or the website of the hotel – but there's much more detailed information in the local newspaper this week. I'll be there so hope to see you all! Now on to other news …

Unit 10, Vocabulary Activity 3

Track 35

1 Could I have a large loaf, please?
2 A bunch of roses, please.
3 Have you got anything that could help with toothache, please?
4 There's a long queue at the checkout – I think we should come back another day.
5 I need a bigger hard drive for my laptop.
6 I'm looking for a sofa to fit my new living room.
7 Half a kilo of sausages, please.
8 I'd like my ring re-sized, please – it's too small.

Unit 10, Vocabulary Activity 5

Track 36

1 **A:** Could I have a large loaf, please?
   B: Of course. Would you like it sliced?

2 **A:** A bunch of roses, please.
   B: Would you like red ones or a mix of red and white?

3 **A:** Have you got anything that could help with toothache, please?
   B: I have these painkillers but you need to see a dentist!

4 **A:** There's a long queue at the checkout – I think we should come back another day.
   B: Oh, now we're here let's do our shopping – it might be better by the time we've finished.

5 **A:** I need a bigger hard drive for my laptop.
   B: Which operating system are you using?

6 **A:** I'm looking for a sofa to fit my new living room.
   B: We have a good choice here. What colour are you interested in?

7 **A:** Half a kilo of sausages, please.
   B: Certainly. These are on special offer today – and they're very tasty.

8 **A:** I'd like my ring re-sized, please - it's too small.
   B: Just a minute and I'll measure your finger.

Unit 10, Grammar Activity 3

Track 37

1 **A:** Where do you get your hair cut?
   B: At the barber shop on the corner. Do you like it?

2 **A:** How often do you get your car serviced?
   B: Once a year, otherwise I think it's not safe to drive.

3 **A:** Why did you get a tattoo done?
   B: I don't know. I just thought it looked good.

4 **A:** How old were you when you got your ears pierced?
   B: I haven't had them pierced yet.

5 **A:** When did you get your teeth whitened?
   B: Last month. I brush them well now to keep them looking good.

6 **A:** Where did you get that shirt made?
   B: I bought it online.

7 **A:** How often do you get your eyes tested?
   B: Every year. I think it's a good thing to do.

8 **A:** When did she have her portrait painted?
   B: Last week. The artist was Italian, I think.

Unit 10, Speaking Activity 1

Track 38

A: Well, if I wanted to sell some things, I definitely wouldn't do it on the internet.

B: Why not? Do you think it's too risky?

A: Yes, I mean, what if you don't get your money?

B: I'm not sure but I think the goods are usually sent after the money has been received.

A: I see. But how are you paid?

B: I think they use something called PayPal. It's quite safe or, at least, that's what I've been told. I've never used it.

A: I've heard about that. You have to set up an account or something. I don't have one so I think it would be better to sell my things at a flea market.

B: You could be right but I think you'd get more money for the things on Cyberbuy.

A: Well, perhaps for the jacket. But I think it would be better to sell the books at the market. What do you think about the newspaper advertisement as a way of selling things?

B: Maybe this is just me but I don't look at newspaper advertisements at all. Do you?

A: I suppose not, now I come to think of it. What about the painting? It looks quite valuable so I wouldn't want to risk taking that to the market. It might get damaged.

B: That's a good point. I would try selling that on Cyberbuy too. A friend of mine sells paintings on the internet and he makes quite a lot of money.

Unit 11, Listening Activity 1

Track 39

1 Which activity does the girl decide to do?

A: So what are you going to do today?

B: There's so much to choose from! I loved the tennis lesson last week but my arm is a bit sore today. The aerobics class is always very good. When I do that I always feel fantastic afterwards, so that's a really good option. Though it's so hot today I'm not sure whether I'd really enjoy it. I'm going on holiday next month so it would be a good idea to improve my scuba diving skills before then – so I guess I'll do that.

A: I think I'll join you!

2 Which photograph are they talking about?

A: That's a great photo! When was it taken?

B: Last year, on holiday, when we visited this brilliant castle. It was meant to be a day out with the whole family, including Mum and Dad though Gran decided not to come as it was very hot.

A: I can't see your sister.

B: That's because she was taking the photo! And Dad had just gone round the corner to buy tickets for us all to get in to the castle – he's in photos we took later, though.

3 When will the new leisure centre open officially?

A: Tell us about the new leisure centre – is it open yet?

B: We're all thrilled that it's finally finished! Building work started a year ago and although it seems a long time, the facilities we're providing are excellent, including a state-of-the-art pool. We're holding a special preview day for families to come and see all the activities on offer for free on 15 July, although the official opening day is not until 20 July. People can register for membership of the centre from 16 July. There will be special discounts for anyone who signs on for a two-year membership, and for people over 65.

4 How will the family travel to their holiday destination this year?

A: Are you looking forward to the holiday?

B: I really am! We try to do something different every year, not like some people who always go back to the same place and do the same things. Two years ago we went camping, and cycled to the camp site. It took us two days to get there but it was really great. This time we'd planned to go to the beach by bus because it's better for the environment, but Gran is coming with us so it'll have to be the car after all.

A: Oh well, next year you can do something different!

5 What does the man decide to eat for lunch?

A: So what would you like?

B: I quite like the look of the steak, though I did have it yesterday. What kind of pasta is it?

A: Pasta with tomatoes and salad – and cheese, of course.

B: Hmm … I'm not so keen on tomatoes, though I do like salad. And it's good for me! I'd really like the burger, though I don't want the chips. I'm trying to lose weight. Maybe I'd better stick to my first choice.

A: How would you like it cooked?

6 What did the girl like best about being on holiday?

A: So what was the best thing about your holiday?

B: Everything was fantastic! I bought loads of things. There were so many souvenirs that were hand-made and great for presents. I got a beautiful vase for my gran. It was a lovely resort too, though I didn't spend much time taking photographs – it was actually too hot! When I'm at home, I don't get much time just to walk in the countryside, so that was what really made the holiday for me. I can't wait to go back!

7 When will the plane take off?

We apologise for the delay in the departure of flight 502 to New York, scheduled for 16.40. This is due to the late arrival of the incoming flight, which will now land at 17.00. Passengers should wait in the departure lounge until called to the boarding gate, which is estimated to be in two hours' time. This means that the new departure time will be 19.30. Once again, we apologise for any inconvenience.

Unit 11, Speaking Activity 1

Track 40

Examiner: Now, I'd like each of you to talk on your own about something. I'm going to give each of you a photograph of people training dogs. Chi, here is your photograph. Please show it to Maria but I'd like you to talk about it. Maria, you just listen. I'll give you your photograph in a moment. Chi, please tell us what you can see in your photograph.

Chi: This photo shows a disabled woman with a dog. They are in the foreground of the photo and in the background, on the left, I can see a house. The dog is wearing a special kind of jacket. It's holding a little basket in its mouth and seems to be offering it to the woman. She might be training the dog to bring her things she needs. The woman is in a wheelchair so I suppose she needs the help of a dog like this. She looks very pleased with the dog. She has something in her hand. It could be some food to give to the dog as a way of telling it that she is pleased. She's probably saying something like, 'Good dog!'

Examiner: Thank you. Now, Maria, here is *your* photograph. It also shows a dog being trained. Please show it to Chi and tell us what you can see in the photograph.

Maria: In this photograph I can see a man training a dog. On their right there seems to be a fire and in the background there are a lot of other people. Just behind them there is another dog. I can't see very clearly but I think some of the people might be firefighters or police because they seem to be wearing uniforms. Also in the top right-hand corner I can see a kind of truck. It could be a fire engine. The man seems to be teaching the dog how to behave in a dangerous situation like a fire. He is watching the dog's reactions to the fire very carefully. It is important for dogs that work helping to rescue people to keep calm and not get frightened in situations like these.

Examiner: Thank you.

Unit 12, Listening Activity 1

Track 41

Michael: Hi, Sara. Did you see that programme on television last night – that one about people with different talents? It was called *Special Talents*.

Sara: Yes, I did, and I thought it was very interesting. It wasn't that I thought what the people could do was extreme or even particularly unexpected, really. What I noticed was that all the people thought they were nothing special – what they could do was normal. I liked that.

Michael: Yes. The programme seemed to say that although we all have natural talents, we don't all bother to recognise them and use them. I thought that was probably true, and it's a pity.

Sara: Imagine if great musicians of the past left their talents undeveloped – people like Beethoven, for example. His music was so beautiful! And the most incredible thing is that he was deaf and couldn't even hear it! A lot of people find that hard to believe.

Michael: Or sports people. After all, isn't being able to run 100 metres in under ten seconds pretty amazing too? And that's something most people can't do.

Sara: I think that even talented people need to have support, otherwise they won't be successful. If they don't, they might give up or never get to the top.

Michael: I'm not sure. Maybe true talent will always get to the top. I don't mean people with strange abilities – you know they do bizarre things like pull a train with their teeth. I mean people with real talent and skill.

Sara: Well, although I agree, I've got a friend who has an amazing musical ability. If she hears a song once, she can just sit down at the piano and play it perfectly. I think we can all do amazing things with the right support!

Unit 12, Speaking Activity 1

Track 42

Maria: So what do you think?

Petros: Well, a cigarette lighter would be good. I don't know what the candle or the dog biscuits are for though.

Maria: Maybe the dog biscuits are in case you need food. If you were lost for several days, you would get very hungry. You need to eat to keep your energy levels up.

Petros: But you can eat the chocolate bar if you were hungry. It's much nicer to eat than a dog biscuit. Ugh!

Maria: I think that's the problem. You might decide to eat the chocolate bar too soon. And then you'd have nothing to eat if you got lost. I know dog biscuits are pretty disgusting but they're probably very nutritious. What do you think about the candle? Would that be useful?

Petros: Maybe but if the cigarette lighter didn't work, the candle had not been any good. Plasters are important.

Maria: Yes, I would definitely put the plasters in and the antiseptic wipes. If someone had a cut or scratch, we would need to clean the wound before we put the plaster on.

Petros: Water purifying tablets are important too. What are the crayons for? We don't have any time to draw pictures if we were lost!

Maria: No, probably not. But we could use them to make marks on trees or rocks. If they sent out a search party for us, they would be able to see where we had been.

Unit 12, Vocabulary Activity 2

Track 43

1 I was racing along the track when I slipped and fell. I twisted my ankle, which was very painful.

2 I was sitting on my board waiting for a big wave but when it came, it was so big that I fell off!

3 I was playing a doubles match with three friends but it started raining and we had to stop because the grass got wet and slippery on the court.

4 I first started walking short distances but I loved it and bought all the right equipment. Now I go for very long treks with friends and it's great exercise.

PRACTICE TEST Paper 2, Listening Part I

Track 44

Example **Where are the woman's car keys?**

A: I can't find my car keys. Can you help me find them?

B: I think they were in your room last night. I remember seeing them on the chest of drawers. Maybe they're still there.

A: I didn't see them when I went up there just now. And I've looked on the kitchen table – I often leave them there but no luck. And they're not in the car either. Oh here they are! I forgot I put them in my bag after breakfast!

1 What time does the film start?

A: What time do you think we should meet before the film?

B: Well, my bus won't get to the town centre before late afternoon, though we don't have to pick the tickets up from the box office until 7.30. The programme doesn't actually begin until 8.15. Let's meet at 6, then we can have a quick meal and get to the cinema in good time.

A: Fine with me.

2 What is the man waiting for?

A: I wish the postman would come soon.

B: Why? You got that parcel yesterday in the post.

A: I know. That was the new books I ordered online. There should have been a postcard as well from my friend. She's away on holiday but the post is very slow from Australia! Perhaps it will come tomorrow. I'm expecting a letter from my sister today. She's sending me a cheque for my birthday next week. I'm looking forward to spending it!

3 What is the date of the anniversary dinner?

It's my parent's wedding anniversary this weekend. Can you believe that they've been married for 30 years? We cooked a meal at home for their 29th anniversary last year but we're all going out for a big dinner at a restaurant on Saturday. That's the 21st, although the anniversary itself is on Monday the 23rd. Not everyone can come then though because of work.

4 What is the man going to do on holiday?

A: What are you going to do for your holiday this year? I thought you were going to the beach.

B: I did that last year but I found lying around doing nothing very boring, so I'm going walking in the Italian lakes this year. I think other things like cycling are just too much exercise for me when I'm on holiday!

A: I know what you mean – though I like winter holidays myself.

5 What is the woman having problems with at the moment?

A: What's the matter? You look angry!

B: Oh, lots of things. Everything seems to be going wrong and it's very expensive to get them fixed! First it was the fridge. It wasn't keeping things cold enough but it's all right now, luckily. Then the television stopped working last night and I'm waiting for the engineer to come. I expect the computer will be the next thing to have a problem, although it hasn't happened yet!

6 What does the girl decide to buy?

A: So what are you going to spend your birthday money on?

B: Well, I'm not sure. My mum has suggested loads of things but I can't decide. I thought about a DVD but they're cheaper to borrow or download. I think I'll just get a new T-shirt – that's always useful!

A: You play a lot of computer games, don't you? What about one of those?

B: No, they're so expensive.

7 What does the woman want to do?

A: I'm quite tired. Let's not go to the cinema tonight.

B: I was looking forward to the film but, OK, we can go tomorrow.

A: You know what? I'd like to go home and watch a DVD. That would be relaxing.

B: What about going out to a restaurant?

A: I'm not hungry and I certainly don't want to do anything too tiring.

PRACTICE TEST, Paper 2
Listening
Part 2

Track 45

Interviewer: Sarah, you're a librarian in a language school. What kind of books do students read?

Sarah: They don't have much time to read – they're busy with their studies! That's why I'm keen on reading in general, not just what they read in class. I encourage them to read at home, in the evenings or at weekends. Students don't always realise that reading for pleasure is one of the best ways of improving their language – and it's easy to do!

Interviewer: Is it hard for students to choose a book?

Sarah: Students often choose an English book because they think it's good for them. And, of course, they don't enjoy it! You have to find something that is interesting for you personally. If you don't like reading science fiction in your own language, you won't like it in English! There is often a DVD of the book too – that's a great way of learning a language. That's why I keep DVDs in the library, although the book comes first.

Interviewer: Is it useful for students to read English books that have been made easier?

Sarah: Of course, but sometimes students choose one because it looks difficult, thinking they'll learn more quickly. But that's not the right way to learn new vocabulary. It might take so long to check the meanings of new words that it becomes boring and they give up. It's not a bad thing to read lots of books that are quite easy – it helps with writing as well because you see how a story is put together.

Interviewer: What books do you personally recommend for students?

Sarah: There's one book which is actually fantasy, called *Time Flies*. Students love it because it mixes a thrilling story with romance, and they can use their own imagination. It's the writer's first book but I'm sure he'll become well-known. This kind of story is good because it's completely different from what students read on their course.

Interviewer: What do you enjoy most about your job?

Sarah: It's great having contact with students. I love talking to them about the different countries they come from. Travelling is one of my hobbies, and I have a list of places I want to visit. But I became a librarian because I've always enjoyed reading and though I can't read much when I'm working, I do get to find out about writers I didn't know about. That's the best thing for me.

Interviewer: Do you think people will read books in the future?

Sarah: Reading is popular now – and not only for study! I know with technology people don't always read paperbacks; some students read on electronic tablets or even on mobile phones, which seems hard – the screen's so small! But I don't think people will ever be bored with stories, and that's very positive for books.

Interviewer: Thanks, Sarah.

PRACTICE TEST Paper 2,
Listening
Part 3

Track 46

Hello, everyone! It's great to welcome you all to the holiday resort! I'm Jonas Watson and I work for Great Sailing Holidays. It's my job to make sure that you have a wonderful time. My office is next to the reception desk, which is at the front of the hotel, and I am there Monday to Friday morning from 9 to 10, and every evening from 6 to 8 apart from Wednesday.

In your rooms, you will find information about the hotel. Breakfast starts at 7 every morning and finishes at 10 but it gets busy around 8 to 8.30, so it's better to eat before or after that time. As you will be sailing all day, you can collect sandwiches for lunch at 9 every morning from the kitchen. Dinner starts at 7.30 and is self-service, so you can eat when you like.

Now to the most important part of your holiday: the sailing. Tomorrow we will all meet at the beach near the hotel at 10.15, where we will give you your first lesson in sailing. I know some of you have sailed before but it is a good idea to go over some basic information again before you go out on your own. You will also find a leaflet in your rooms about staying safe on the water. You can read that this evening. We want you to enjoy yourselves but also to be safe! So before you start, make sure that you have a lifejacket. You can collect one from my office after this meeting. Some general rules: find out about the weather before you go out in the boat, and tell someone where you are going and what time you expect to be back. Don't forget to take sun cream, a hat and a bottle of water with you – it can get hot out on the water. Right. That's all for now – unless anyone has any questions?

PRACTICE TEST Paper 2,
Listening
Part 4

Track 47

Steve: Hi, Janet. Did you see the latest part of *Dancing Star* last night? I was really looking forward to it but then I had so much homework to do that I couldn't watch it live. I recorded it, though, so I'll watch it tonight.

Janet: That was unlucky! I won't tell you what happened then.

Steve: No, please don't. Though I don't think I'll be able to get through the day without someone giving it away!

Janet: Probably! It was great! I couldn't stop thinking about it afterwards. I rang my friend Sue just to talk about it! There are only four dancers left in the competition now and one of them will get a contract with a dance company.

Steve: I know – that's a great prize. Though there's a lot of hard work involved in being a professional dancer. So many try to do it and aren't successful. I used to dance so I know how it is. Anyone is brave to go in for a competition like this.

Janet: That's true. And I thought some of the dancers weren't really very good in the first few programmes but now it's a real chance for the good ones to show what they can do. I think being on television like this is a great opportunity for them. Did you ever think about doing it yourself?

Steve: Not me! The judges are really unkind in their comments. They say exactly what they think and they're not very nice. I think it would make me feel bad.

Janet: But they have to be honest. Though I agree they do say horrible things about the people sometimes – stuff about what they look like. That's got nothing to do with whether they can dance and I don't like that.

Steve: I think I'll just be me – keep on doing what I can do. I don't want to be famous! Though I suppose it might have some advantages – like money!

Janet: Well, wait until you've seen the programme. Then you can tell me what you think about the result.

PRACTICE TEST Paper 3, Speaking Part 1

Track 48

Now, what's your name?

Thank you. What's your surname?

How do you spell it?

Where do you live?

Do you work or are you a student?

Do you enjoy watching television?

What did you do last weekend?

What do you enjoy doing with your friends in the evenings?

Where will you go on holiday in the summer?

PRACTICE TEST Paper 3, Speaking Part 2

Track 49

In the next part you are going to talk to each other. I'm going to describe a situation to you:

A friend from England is going to spend three weeks in your country. Talk together about the things she will need to have with her in your country and decide which are the most important things for her to have with her.

I'll say that again: A friend from England is going to spend three weeks in your country. Talk together about the things she will need to have with her in your country and decide which are the most important things for her to have with her. All right? Talk together.

PRACTICE TEST Paper 3, Speaking Part 3

Track 50

Now, I'd like each of you to talk on your own about something. I'm going to give each of you a photograph of people travelling on holiday. Candidate A, here is your photograph. Please show it to Candidate B, but I'd like you to talk about it. Candidate B, you just listen. I'll give you your photograph in a moment.

Candidate A, please tell us what you can see in your photograph.

Thank you. Now, Candidate B, here is your photograph. It also shows people travelling on holiday. Please show it to Candidate A and tell us what you can see in the photograph.

Thank you.

PRACTICE TEST Paper 3, Speaking Part 4

Track 51

Your photographs showed people travelling on holiday. Now I'd like you to talk together about the different ways you like to travel when you are on holiday, and the ways you don't like to travel.

Thank you. That's the end of the test.

Pearson Education Limited
Edinburgh Gate
Harlow
Essex CM20 2JE
England
and Associated Companies throughout the world.

www.pearsonelt.com

First published 2013

Sixth impression 2018

ISBN: 978-1-4479-0736-7 (Gold Preliminary Exam Maximiser with key)

Set in Myriad Pro
Printed in Slovakia by Neografia

Acknowledgements

The publishers and author(s) would like to thank the following people and institutions for their feedback and comments during the development of the material: Daniela Donati (Italy), Diana Pena (Mexico), Michael Smith (Spain), Pauline Bokhari, Pat Chappell, Sue Ireland (UK).

Photographs:
The publisher would like to thank the following for their kind permission to reproduce their photographs:
(Key: b-bottom; c-centre; l-left; r-right; t-top)
Alamy Images: ableimages 61, Eric Audras / PhotoAlto 23, Carolyn Clarke 24, John Cooper 97/8, Ian Dagnall 29, DAJ / amana images inc. 97/10, FirstShot 71, EWING GALLOWAY / ClassicStock 28b, Dennis Hallinan 42, HD57life 97/6, IS098Q296 / Image Source 10/5, Mike Kemp / RubberBall 18, Helmut Meyer zur Capellen / imagebroker 17, Jason Stitt 39, Peter Titmuss 112b, UpperCut Images 97/9, Richard Wear / Design Pics Inc. 13t, szefei wong 10/2, Wig Worland 36, sandy young 51; **Corbis:** Image Source 55b, Daniel Sicolo / Design Pics 101, Atsuko Tanaka / Bridge 55t; **Fotolia.com:** andersphoto 30/1, BortN66 30/5, CandyBox Images 13b, cedrov 30/8, Ruslan Kudrin 30/4, Anna Lurye 30/6, Gordana Sermek 30/7; **Getty Images:** Biddiboo / Photographer's Choice 34/1, Brian Cassella / Chicago Tribune / MCT 70t, db2stock 12r, David De Lossy / Photodisc 32b, R. Gates / Archive Photos 28t, Robert Ginn / Photolibrary 66, John Lamb / Photonica 112t, Kevin Mazur / WireImage 49t, Ryan McVay / Lifesize 34/3, Shalom Ormsby / Blend Images 58b, Doris Rudd Designs, Photography / Flickr 12l, Paul Simcock / UpperCut Images 56/4, Zave Smith / Workbook Stock 10/4, Geoff Tompkinson / Taxi 58t, Betsie Van Der Meer / Taxi 32t; **Pearson Education Ltd:** Jon Barlow. Pearson Education Ltd 97/7, MindStudio. Pearson Education Ltd 34/4, Studio 8. Pearson Education Ltd 10/3, Weststock. Photodisc 100, Coleman Yuen. Pearson Education Asia Ltd 30/2, 30/3; **Rex Features:** Beretta / Sims 48, 49b, PAUL WATTS 70b; **Shutterstock.com:** Ermolaev Alexander 33, amidala76 70c, AVAVA 56/5, Bryan Busovicki 73, Natalia Dobryanskaya 47, evgenymate 56/2, Paul Fleet 25, oliveromg 30b, shyshak roman 34/2, Jason Stitt 34/5, Supri Suharjoto 10/1, Mathieu Viennet 056/1, Lisa F. Young 56/3

All other images © Pearson Education

In some instances we have been unable to trace the owners of copyright material, and we would appreciate any information that would enable us to do so.

Illustrated by Oxford Designers and Illustrators